Tips and Tricks
for Web Site Managers

Mark Kerr
Editor

Routledge
Taylor & Francis Group

LONDON AND NEW YORK

INFORMATION MANAGEMENT

First published 2001 by ASLIB-IMI

Published 2015 by Routledge
2 Park Square, Milton Park, Abingdon, Oxon OX14 4RN
711 Third Avenue, New York, NY 10017, USA

*Routledge is an imprint of the Taylor & Francis Group,
an informa business*

Information Management International (IMI) is a trading name of Aslb.

Aslib-IMI provides consultancy and information services, professional development training, conferences, specialist recruitment, Internet products, publishes journals (in hard copt and electronic formats), books and directories and provides outsourcing services to the information community.

Aslib-IMI, founded in 1924, is a world class corporate membership organisation with over 2,000 members in some 70 countries. Aslib actively promotes best practice in the management of information resources. It lobbies on all aspects of the management of, and legislation concerning, information at local, national and international levels.

ISBN 13: 978-0-85142-439-2 (pbk)

Contents

Acknowledgements

This book has only been possible with the generous co-operation and enthusiastic participation of over 60 contributors. The case studies and tips and tricks were provided by a wide range of experts and practitioners, who are listed below, and I would like to express my heartfelt thanks to them all for sharing their knowledge and experience for this book.

Particular thanks go to Alison Scammell, commissioning editor at Aslib, for her enthusiasm and support during this book's development and for the occasional nudge when deadlines approached in their usual unexpected way. Thanks also to Sue Bourner for copy-editing a collection of pages into this final version, and for smoothing out many wrinkles along the way.

A final acknowledgement is to all those web sites and web site creators who have provided resources for others and to those whose web sites instruct simply by being examples of good design. This generosity of spirit is what makes the Web such a welcoming and encouraging environment.

Case Studies *(in alphabetical order of organisation)*

BBC Betsie: Wayne Myers

Cambridge University Press: Ivan Salcedo

Countrybookshop.co.uk: Geraldine Rose and Sridhar Gowda

Dotgain: Paul James

EARL: Linda Berube and Sally Chambers with Godfrey Oswald

EEVL: Linda Kerr and Roddy MacLeod

Institute of Actuaries: Sally Grover and Emma Pegg

Motley Fool: George Row

National Gallery: Simon Crab and David Hart

OUT-LAW.COM: Struan Robertson

Tips and Tricks *(in alphabetical order of contributor)*

The following people generously shared their top tips:

Kylie Baxter, School of Law, University of Hull; Oliver Bond, Dotgain; Judith Bonser, Onion Productions; Gary Catchpole, Creative Director, Eye Design; Mike Chivhanga, Web Development Consultant, Internet Studies Research Group, City University; Liz Citron, MD, Arehaus; Peter Cochrane, Chief Technologist, BT; Pam Davies, Leeds University Library; Professor Mark Elsom-Cook, School of Computing and Mathematics, University of Northumbria; William Hann, Managing Editor, FreePint; Sam Hutchinson, shockedesign; David King, Dudley College; Doreen Louvre, REFUND Project, University of Newcastle upon Tyne; Mike Lowndes, Web Manager, Natural History Museum; Beccy Manley, KidStuff; Elliott Manley, MoltenGold; Matt Martell, ContentGenerators; Marieke Napier, Information Officer, UKOLN and Editor, *Exploit Interactive* and *Cultivate Interactive* web magazines; Neil Pawley, Consultant, open.gov.uk; John Pullam, McLean Systems Inc.; Harriet Ridolfo, Bournemouth University; Gillian Roach, Editor, *Internet Works* magazine; Elaine Robinson, Freelance Web Developer; Mike Scott, Web Developer, BBC News Online; George Edw. Seymour, Systems Information Resources; Eddie Stewart, Web Master, DERA; David Supple, External Relations and Development Office, Birmingham University.

Trademarks

Introduction

You need help. Whatever type of web site you manage, you need help. Sometimes you don't need very much help, and just a hint will do, but sometimes you need blue flashing lights and sirens and a full emergency team of assistants. This book is intended to sit somewhere between those two extremes. It might provide the occasional hint here and there or it might have the information you need to avoid a full-scale emergency.

It is not intended to be a full-blown HTML or web design manual, nor does it presume to replace the acquisition of experience and knowledge over time. I do hope that it will be useful as a source book of ideas and suggestions, both to improve and enhance the performance and appearance of a site, and to assist in the 'behind-the-scenes' management that most web sites require.

Thanks to the generosity of the contributors, this book includes two types of expert advice: case studies and tips and tricks.

The case studies provide an insight into the way in which several well-known organisations have designed and developed their web sites. The organisations cover the spectrum from large to small, public to private sector, academic to commercial, and between them they deal with many of the key issues involved in designing, developing and maintaining a web site.

The tips and tricks are the essential nuggets of information that you pick up almost by accident at the water fountain, on a training course, at a conference, or simply chatting with colleagues. Any single tip might save you hours of effort, or help you avoid a critical error, and put together they provide you with the equivalent of several years of hard-won experience at the coalface of web development.

The book has been organised into six key sections, and the tips and tricks are located wherever they are most relevant. Most of the case studies, however, cover more than a single issue, so I have grouped them into two sections the first loosely covering general design issues, the second (equally loosely) covering structural and management issues.

The supporting web site (http://www.webtipsandtricks. com) provides links to the sites used in case studies, as well as to the partners, tools and resources referred to throughout the book. This site will be maintained and expanded, and I welcome suggestions and additions to make the site as useful as possible to the web site management community.

Chapter 1

Site Definition and Planning

Researching the marketing and publishing environment, assessing the competition and planning the web site design process – all these activities are essential if you are to give your web site project the greatest chance of success, at the least cost to you and your organisation.

Planning

Whether the aim is to develop a new web site or improve an existing service, it is increasingly clear that many sites do not always meet their targets. These targets may be revenue based or they may be more abstract, seeking to present the organisation as effectively and efficiently as possible to its audience.

The publicly available Web is developing at breathtaking speed. A recent report from Cyveillance (http://www.cyveillance.com) estimated that 7,000,000 new pages are added to the Web each day. The current total size of the public Web is over two billion documents. No matter what the content, purpose or location of your site, at some level you are competing with much of this information for the attention of your existing or anticipated audience. Developing an effective service to achieve your objectives requires a strategy; and an effective strategy requires a plan.

There are four basic stages through which the planner has to move to create an effective project plan:

- Awareness
- Familiarity
- Understanding
- Readiness.

Awareness

Although your site may be designed by other staff, or by an outside contractor, it is essential that you, as the site manager, understand the

'Research till you drop. When setting up a web site or e-business do as much research as you can to find out who is offering similar services on-line (and off-line). Use search engines, company lists, newsgroups and word of mouth to get as much information on your competitors as you possibly can. And don't just limit your research to European companies – EVERYONE is a competitor on-line. Most importantly, don't stop researching once your e-company/dotcom is off the ground. Carry on researching and refining.'

Gillian Roach
Editor, *Internet Works* magazine

broad principles of site design so that the correct decisions can be made at the outset. Many of the readers of this book are not designers but managers, who will be hiring in the designers or managing the web team. Just understanding the jargon and the basic principles of web design can go a long way towards preventing misunderstandings by the designers about your requirements.

Familiarity

There are as many methods for designing web sites as there are designers, but use of a simple methodology, and available tools, can avoid confusion and a lack of clarity in the design, purpose and presentation of the site. A relentless pursuit of the cutting edge of design and development can mean that nobody is actually comfortable with the tools being used, and everybody is learning new possibilities all the time. At one level that can generate a highly creative environment and a stimulating atmosphere, but on the other hand there does need to be some stability if the web site is expected to perform reliably on a day-to-day basis.

Understanding

If you understand your requirements you will be better placed to communicate, monitor and implement them. Conversely, if you have only a limited grasp of the medium, how it will affect your organisation and how you intend to use it, then it will be difficult – even impossible – to communicate your needs clearly and accurately to the design and development team.

Building a Subject Information Gateway Team

'Subject information gateways are increasingly becoming a popular and an effective way to assemble and repackage information and make it accessible from one single point of entry. The gateway will indeed be a useful starting point to search the web both for novice and experienced users. The success of the gateway is highly dependent on the relevance of the content, and this is determined well before the gateway is built.

One of the best ways to ensure the success of a gateway is to have an interdisciplinary web development team. The team should obviously include technical staff and subject experts who will act as content editors and providers. It should also consist of beneficiaries of the web resource itself, who may not necessarily be professionals but ordinary people.

Carrying out an information-needs assessment before building the gateway, during the building of the resource and after the gateway has been launched will ensure that it continues to be an effective information service. It might even be advisable to carry out on-line focus studies with the target audience.'

Mike Chivhanga
Web Development Consultant,
Internet Studies Research Group,
City University

Readiness

Like many processes, the design of a web site can be broken down into simple steps, and each step can then be further broken down in to tasks and actions. This book is based on the principle that most large projects can be reduced to 'bite-sized chunks', thus reducing the fear factor and avoiding the sense of being overwhelmed by the gargantuan nature of the task ahead. Creating an action plan, setting achievable targets within sensible deadlines, and distributing responsibility appropriately, will ensure that the project moves forwards as smoothly as possible.

The Five-Step Doodle

It's not strikingly original, but it's true nonetheless, to say that the best planning tools a web site manager has are a simple piece of paper and a pencil. The ability to sketch out a site structure, to visualise the relationship between different areas of content, to demonstrate information flow and to create understandable page layouts – all these require an initial doodle.

The doodle is vastly underrated as a professional tool, but one common design factor links every great web site – they probably all started as a bit of a doodle.

Sit down with a piece of paper, and create a few short lists:

- Identify **outcomes**
- Picture the potential areas of **content**
- Imagine the information a **visitor** to the web site might want or expect
- List the **departments** in your organisation that might want to be represented on your web site
- Identify the key elements on your **competitors'** web sites.

Outcomes

There are many potential site outcomes, but essentially they are divided between internal and external results. Internal outcomes might include satisfying your organisation's core mission, justifying a departmental budget or staffing level, or reducing costs in delivery of information and services. External outcomes might include providing new outlets for your products, information or services through customer acquisition and increased sales value, or raising awareness of your organisation in the wider marketing environment.

Content

The range of content expected and available from your web site is assessed more closely in Chapter 2, but it includes corporate and service information as well as customer support.

Visitor Expectations

If your site is supporting an existing service you will have a reasonably clear idea of what your users expect from you, and therefore – in theory at least – what they expect from your web site.

Departmental Expectations

Overlook internal expectations at your peril – the needs of your organisation cannot always be described in terms of customer service. Other agendas, hidden or explicit, are an unavoidable part of an institutional web site. It may simply be a matter of reflecting internal structure and relationships, but making this compatible with an outward-looking site is no trivial matter.

> 'Keep putting yourself in the user's position. They have no idea about what is in your site or how to get there. Give them some pointers. Think very hard about why people would want to come to your site and what they would like to get out of it.'
>
> **Liz Citron**
> **MD, Arehaus**

Competitor Elements

Your web site may have a clear mission, relevant and sufficient content, be focused on customer service and reflect internal organisational needs, but there is one more element to consider – the competition. The transparent nature of the Web provides you with the opportunity to monitor those sites that are competing for your visitors' attention. Identify elements that enhance these sites, and consider developing alternatives for your own site. This does not mean simply copying, but it does mean ensuring that you do not lose competitive advantage due to simple ignorance of the competitive environment. Even unique sites have to compete for users' time and attention.

Each of these steps may result in a short list of one or two items, or a much more extensive one. When you've finished, stop and look at these five lists. Do they match each other? Probably not. It is very unlikely that what *you* (the company) have to say is the same as what *they* (the audience) want to see. The Web is a publishing and communication medium, and as such it needs to be focused on the audience. This will be a recurring theme throughout this book, but it is surprising how often this is overlooked, particularly in information-based sites.

Of course, it is not compulsory for your doodle to actually be a doodle – it could just as usefully be the outcome of a series of lengthy committee meetings, or the product of a consultancy project. You might need to use the full range of research tools, including focus groups, customer interviews and desk research. The important result is the comparison and reconciliation between producer and audience expectations in such a way that you achieve your intended aims.

Research

As with any strategic development, you should conduct some basic market research prior to the site development. This will help keep your planning process focused on the customer and demonstrate that you are aware of the wider environment in which your site exists. There are many research tools and services on the Web that can assist you with this process.

Who's on the Web?

Everyone and anyone seem to be using the Web as their primary source of external communication, from governments and large corporations to small corner shops, local charities and individuals. A simple analysis of the currently registered domains shows the distribution of domains by type.

Domain name registrations at 7 October 2000	
Type of domain name	**Number registered**
All domains	30,656,015
.com	18,563,619
.net	3,441,823
.org	2,172,710
.edu	5,673
.gov	730
.uk (United Kingdom)	2,213,596
.de (Germany)	2,032,197
.au (Australia)	151,148
.it (Italy)	341,005
.ar (Argentine)	353,548
.nl (Netherlands)	443,272
.br (Brazil)	312,115

Source: DomainStats (http://www.domainstats.com)

The UK figures can be broken down further using Nominet's statistics.

UK domain name statistics at 31 August 2000	
Type of domain name	Number registered
.co.uk	1,980,135
.org.uk	126,225
.ltd.uk	7887
.plc.uk	1328
.net.uk	489
.sch.uk	20,828
Total	2,137,199

Source: Nominet (http://www.nominet.org.uk)

For organisations creating a new brand, or launching themselves on to the Web for the first time, the selection of an effective domain name can be a difficult process. All the 'good' names seem to have gone, and the organisation's preferred domain name might have been taken by someone with no apparent claim to that name. Trademark and copyright issues aside, choosing a domain name is often simpler than many organisations think: the most important aspects are that it should be memorable, and easy to spell and type. Issues relating to brand reinforcement and literal, descriptive names are secondary, and can be dealt with by effective marketing and explanatory text on the site or promotional literature. The name should be linguistically simple, meaning that when you tell someone your domain name over the telephone you should not have to spell it out carefully, explaining hyphens or underscores. Simplicity is all. Avoid punctuation and clever spelling tricks – *in4mation* for **information** or *content4u* for **contentforyou** – may look very clever, but you will have to explain them carefully every single time. And just because you can now have a domain name that's up to 63 characters long, it doesn't mean that it's a good idea!

If you are determined to register your domain in several overseas territories, a search on NetNames (http://www.netnames.co.uk) produces a table of all the national domains, showing whether a particular name is available or in use. At the very least you should check to see if 'your' domain is being registered by companies who could confuse your visitors as to their identity and purpose, whether by accident or by design. Users who guess a URL rather than doing a search could find themselves in some very unexpected places. One famous example is the White House domain: www.whitehouse.gov is the official Web site for the White House, but www.whitehouse.net is a spoof site put up by a Washington Internet company, and www.whitehouse.com was registered by a company offering adult material. Guessing the domain in circumstances like these can be hazardous. In particular, well-known organisations or companies need to be aware of companies registering sound-a-like names or misspellings to draw unwary visitors to their own advertising-laden pages. For example, www.amason.co.uk is a page linked through an affiliate link to the WH Smith on-line bookstore.

Multiple registrations (in different country domains) may be appropriate for organisations with strong global brands, but an organisation with a strong UK-specific brand, particularly one where the UK location is central to the organisation's image and service, even if it operates overseas or has international visitors or users, may not find this as essential.

If you need to know more about the 'average' Internet user, Nua (http://www.nua.ie/surveys/) provides research reports and statistics on user behaviour and web site activity by collecting and redistributing press releases and executive summaries from an enormous range of market research companies. Commerce and retail market research reports, social and demographic data, technical information on browsers and operating systems – all are freely available and searchable. Nua also collects and consolidates national Internet user surveys from around the world to come up with 'the big number' of the global Internet population, ideal for persuading sceptical management that the Internet is an appropriate strategic development for an organisation.

Number of Internet users, September 2000	
World	377.65 million
Africa	3.11 million
Asia/Pacific	89.68 million
Europe	105.89 million
Middle East	2.40 million
Canada and USA	161.31 million
Latin America	15.26 million

Source: Nua (http://www.nua.ie/surveys/how_many_online/index.html)

To obtain information about the users of your own web service, you will need access to the server statistics for your site. This is discussed in detail in Chapter 6.

What's Your Site For?

Ask yourself just what your web site is actually for. You may want it to deliver information, promote a message, increase sales, or recruit members – essentially perhaps do everything you do in the real world, but on-line. It may also enable you – or your users – to do things you could not afford to do in the real world. 'What's it for?' can also be read as 'What is it intended to achieve?' which brings us back to intended outcomes. Typically, the intended outcomes for a site are some or all of the following:

- To generate revenue, enquiries or bookings
- To deliver or collect information
- To raise awareness or profile
- To support off-line activities
- To support customers
- To support staff in the delivery of services.

> 'Keep putting yourself in the user's position. They have no idea about what is in your site or how to get there. Give them some pointers. Think very hard about why people would want to come to your site and what they would like to get out of it.'
>
> **Liz Citron**
> **MD, Arehaus**

Who Is Your Core Audience?

Delivering information effectively requires an understanding not only of the information needs of your intended audience, but of the audience themselves.

Internal or External

A captive audience of internal users (members, students, staff, etc.) may be easier to reach in marketing terms, but the content still needs to be relevant to their needs, and the style and structure appropriate for their skill levels. You will normally have a good idea of the technology available to this user group, so you can design around them to

> 'When trying to analyse who you are designing the site for, it's often better to start out by deciding who it is *not* intended for.'
>
> **Professor Mark Elsom-Cook**
> **School of Computing and Mathematics, University of Northumbria**

some extent. A largely external audience will have a wider range of skills, equipment and experience, and so you should consider either working to a lower common denominator or, more usefully, offering additional support for those who need it.

An internal audience might be addressed in two distinct ways: through an external web site, with private sections for information relevant only to internal users; or by an intranet specifically set up to deliver information and services within an organisation. An intranet site might use similar design and communication technology to the Internet site, but restrict access by use of passwords or firewalls (software or hardware that limits access to authorised users). An extranet enables a trusted group of external users – suppliers or distributors for example – to gain limited access to some parts of the intranet site. The table below demonstrates some of the differences between the Internet and intranets and extranets as a communication channel.

	Internet	**Intranet**	**Extranet**
Type of access	Open	Private	Controlled
Type of user	General public	Organisation members	Business partners
Type of information	Marketing, non-confidential	Proprietary, confidential within the organisation	Selective sharing, confidential to the partners

An extranet is often a sub-set of an intranet, with information usually restricted to the intranet being made available to a controlled group of external users – perhaps formal business partners, high-level subscribers or contract staff. The table below shows how information published on an intranet might be filtered for use on an extranet.

Activity	**Intranet**	**Extranet**
Chat-room software	Discussion with employees	Discussions with clients and suppliers
Human resources	All data	Job vacancy information
Legacy applications	View and amend data	View selected data
Pooling information	Among employees	Among partners
Marketing data	View and amend data	Order goods, track progress
Gather information	Solicit employee feedback	Solicit customer feedback

Educational and Age Range
These factors may affect your choice of colours and graphics, even your style of language. A text-heavy page might be informative and convenient for committed and expert readers, but deter younger, more casual or less experienced visitors. A service aimed entirely at experts or senior professionals can afford to use more jargon than one that is also designed to attract new users. Again, designing for the lowest common denominator is not the only solution – but you should consider adding extra information, such as a dictionary, tutorials or help-sheets.

Technical Expertise

Will your users be familiar with the Web, and comfortable with navigational metaphors and plug-ins such as Flash and Acrobat, or will they require very explicit instructions? If your site relies on documents in PDF format, or extensive database manipulation, will the users be able to cope? Potential problems such as these may be solved simply by providing clear and well-signposted help pages. Dumbing-down the entire output is absolutely not a requirement, but aiding those less proficient most certainly is.

If you decide to proclaim 'suitable for version 4 or above of Netscape and Internet Explorer' at least be able and prepared to demonstrate that this choice is based on market and audience awareness, and not on the designer's laziness.

With an internal audience – institutional, membership or intranet – you have a little more power to specify the technology they should use to access your information, but there will always be peripheral users who may be unable or unwilling to conform to your expectations. Whether your web site can accommodate them may depend on your commitment to inclusiveness. The concepts of inclusiveness and accessibility are discussed in greater detail in Chapter 4.

Building the Team

Few individuals have the time or the ability to learn all the skills necessary to create, manage and maintain a web site. Larger web sites in particular will involve a number of people with different areas of expertise, each contributing to the team. The requirements can be divided in to several key areas, with strong similarities to a print magazine production team:

- Site production – the practical and technical construction of the pages and features within the site – using e.g. HTML, Perl, JavaScript, dynamic HTML
- Graphic and visual design – developing the visual style and providing the illustrations – using e.g. Photoshop, Flash, Dreamweaver
- Content management – commissioning, editing and updating the textual elements that make up the site
- Project management – managing the project, the staff and the resource acquisition and allocation.

If you manage all the above with just one person, then congratulations – you have discovered multi-tasking! Of course, there are many on-line resources, script archives, graphics libraries and sources of content that ease the pressure of these roles. However large or small your team, it is the teamwork element that remains crucial. Sharing expertise, encouraging ideas, coping with (even welcoming) conflict, managing change – all these skills and abilities are daily requirements for web site managers.

'Advance yourself by advancing others. Let others take the credit if they must. Don't exclude or neglect anyone who wants to be on the bandwagon. Don't be territorial. Accept other people's responsibility. Be reliable. Enable. Become a little pillar of society. Never blow your own trumpet.'

Mike Scott
Web Developer, BBC News Online

It is important to develop an inclusive style of site management that encourages contributions from outside the core team. Encouraging colleagues who are outside the web team to feel a sense of ownership of the site will make recruiting assistance for specific projects and emergencies a good deal easier. The role of the web site manager often involves being less a manager, and more a circus ringmaster or ringmistress.

'Confucius said: "A gentleman is never afraid to end up in the street." Never hang on to your job or compromise your judgement in order to avoid change and uncertainty. There is always another job somewhere for someone able to accept responsibility and willing to start at the bottom. The more one hangs on in the wrong situation, the less employable one becomes.'

Mike Scott
Web Developer, BBC News Online

References and Resources

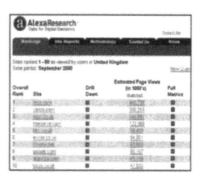

By analysing the web sites visited by users of the Alexa search tool, Alexa Research provides an estimate of the top-50 web sites by traffic in 18 countries. A subscription is required for access to the full statistics, but even without one you can see which sites are the busiest (number of page views) and 'stickiest' (average length of visit, number of pages viewed) in 28 leading Internet national domains.

Source: Alexa Research
(http://www.alexaresearch.com)

 A web content study by Cyveillance announced that 2.1 billion unique, publicly available pages exist on the Internet.

The study also found that the Internet is growing at the explosive rate of more than 7 million pages each day, indicating that it will double in size by early 2001.

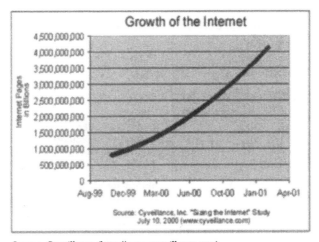

Source: Cyveillance (http://www.cyveillance.com)

Useful Web Sites

DomainStats (http://www.domainstats.com)
  Summary of domain registrations

Nominet (http://www.nominet.org.uk)
  UK domain registrar

NetNames (http://www.netnames.co.uk)
  Domain name reseller

Nua (http://www.nua.ie/surveys/)
  Market research resource

Alexa Research (http://www.alexaresearch.com)
  Top traffic web sites

Cyveillance (http://www.cyveillance.com)
Strategic analysis of web content

WebSnapshot (http://websnapshot.mycomputer.com)
Global web data and trends

Chapter 2

Information Architecture and Navigation Design

Content is only useful if it can be found. A robust information architecture to allow for expansion, and effective navigation to assist in the location of the required information, are both essential if the site is to deliver its information to the user reliably.

Selecting Content and Structure

The planning process should not be limited to new sites. Every web site should be subjected to a constant process of evaluation by its management. While many leading commercial sites are totally redesigned every 12–18 months, this is often impractical or unnecessary for services whose style does not need to change with each new season's fashions. Nevertheless, the principle of continuous development is certainly one that should be applied to all sites.

> 'In a survey of 200 web sites, 43 percent lacked basic navigation aids. Of these, 73 percent did not have text navigation at the bottom of their pages, 27 percent did not have a link back to the home page from all interior pages, 50 percent did not link to the site map from the home page and 39 percent did not have a search tool.'
>
> **Giga Information Group (http://www.gigaweb.com)**

There are a number of design considerations that should be clarified prior to developing or redeveloping a site:

- What is the appropriate style and structure?
- How will the site be created and managed?
- How will the content be managed?

When designing a site, you need to imagine how the visitor will experience your design. There are several styles of site structure and navigation which dictate how the visitor moves from section to section, and this movement is governed by the links and connections you have installed. Whether or not you obey the three-click rule (a widely quoted standard

> 'Make sure that the user can reach everything within three clicks and less than a second speed and convenience transcend graphics and visual design.'
>
> **Peter Cochrane Chief Technologist, BT**

in navigation design, which states that the user should be able to get from the home page to any other page on the site within three clicks of the mouse) may depend on the content and style of your site, but your overriding aim should always be to get visitors to their intended destination as easily and smoothly as possible.

The three styles outlined here – linear, hierarchical and matrix-based – are not exclusive of each other. In practice, a well-designed site will use a combination of these styles. This might include an overall matrix, with a hierarchical system for specific sections and linear sections where relevant. There is no 'ideal' structure, except one that presents your content so that it is clear, attractive and effective.

Although these styles represent a very formalised – perhaps even unrealistic – approach to planning a structure, they do provide a methodology for storyboarding the content of the site. Just as a movie director will storyboard a production, showing key scenes and stunts, so the site storyboard shows key sections and the expected layout of pages within each section. This helps to group the content into the appropriate areas, and enables responsibility for different sections to be divided and delegated as necessary.

Linear Structure

The linear structure describes pages that flow in strict sequence, with the user being directed to follow links such as 'next' and 'previous'. This gives the site manager quite a high degree of control over the behaviour of the visitor, but does not provide a very interactive experience.

This style follows that of a book, where you start at the beginning and generally keep going forwards (perhaps pausing occasionally to look something up in a glossary or the footnotes). Once the end has been reached, that event is closed. While obviously limited, this approach is very appropriate for complex explanations or for demonstrating processes – or just to break up a long document into more manageable pages.

Diversions could still be provided, for example to on-line citations and references, look-up tables, calculating tools and other activities that enhance the understanding of the document.

Hierarchical Structure

The hierarchical structure is typically based on a set of parallel directories, each with sub-directories or sub-menus. This allows much larger amounts of information to be placed within easy reach of the home page, but careful design is needed to avoid confusing the visitor.

Sideways movement between directory areas (particularly at the lower levels) is seen as less necessary, except from top-level pages. This structure is ideal for subjects divided in a similar way to a corporate organisational chart, with distinct subject, function or geographic areas.

Hierarchical structures are also good for zooming in on a subject, as each layer down takes you to more detail. Navigation within directories could be based on a linear structure, but at the upper levels the visitor should be able to 'step across' to other parts of the site. For example, on the BBC news site (http://news.bbc.co.uk) clicking on the 'Business' link takes you to the business news area, where you can see all the articles in that section. You can also move directly to the top level of the health, politics or international news sections – as well as to other top-level parts of the BBC sites – where you can then see all the articles within that topic.

'Plan your site with the future in mind, aiming to use a neat directory structure. Then, by placing an index.htm file in each directory you can have "neat web address shortcuts". For example:
http://www.dudleycol.ac.uk/map/
http://www.dudleycol.ac.uk/courses/
http://www.dudleycol.ac.uk/contact/
http://www.dudleycol.ac.uk/international/'

David King
Dudley College

Matrix-Based Structure

This style implies that there is no strict hierarchy of information or content – it is all as important or as interesting as the rest. The implication is that you can access any part of the site from any other part (note 'part', not necessarily 'individual page').

While this is ideal for most information sites with multiple topics and interests, the navigation is more complex here, as the visitor needs to be able to move up and down within the current area, but also access other areas at will. This is best achieved with consistent directory navigation bars on each page listing the main areas of the site, from which specific pages can then be found.

Hybrid Structure

In practice, of course, most sites employ a combination of styles, and the real value in understanding the structures is in designing the range of navigation options that is going to lead your users around the site.

The purpose of identifying the structure is to enable you to plan out navigation links and – just as importantly – decide where

'Always plan out your structure FIRST, taking into consideration where additional pages could/will appear. Draw yourself a CLEAR structure diagram and fasten it next to your computer. This will allow you to visually map out your site. And don't be afraid to scribble all over it!'

Sam Hutchinson
shockedesign

new and expanded content will be located. Creating new directories and adjusting your structure several months into a project can be time-consuming and confusing.

Information Architecture

The basic requirements of information architecture are simple: information must be collected, labelled and organised in such a way as to be easily retrieved by the end user, who may have no prior knowledge of how it is organised.

Information architecture is sometimes split in to three core elements: metaphor, labelling and navigation.

> 'Analyse where your visitors are going. If they spend 30 seconds on the first two pages, and nine minutes on the third, your site architecture is wrong. The content on page 3 should be moved to page 1.'
>
> **Matt Martell**
> **ContentGenerators**

Metaphor

If you are using a metaphor on your web site (a tree of knowledge, discovery tree, development path, etc.), make it explicit on the home page. Then your users have the initial clue they need to look for relevant elements as they travel through the site. Even without an abstract metaphor it should be clear from the design of the buttons or links whether they will take the user to a page or to a directory, and of course it should be absolutely clear when a graphic is just an illustrative ornament and when it is functioning as a signpost.

Labelling

Make it clear what is behind each link – if you have four buttons labelled 'FAQ', 'About Us', 'History' and 'Background', how are users to know what they mean? They could all be grouped into one section, and explained a little more clearly. Similarly, 'News' or 'What's New' on a site home page implies information of interest to the end user, but all too often it is simply what is new in the organisation, or on the site, rather than in the world at large. The information is valid, it's just the label that is unclear. Call it 'Company News' or 'Site News' and the possibility of confusion is minimised.

Navigation

Navigation design combines site structure with clearly labelled links and effective search tools: this can make the difference between a site being usable and unusable. The

> 'Remember, your users will never view your site the same way as you do. Before going live with a site always try out your menu structure on a group of tame users who have not previously seen the site.'
>
> **Eddie Stewart**
> **Web Master, DERA**

design targets are fast access to information from the home page, and easy location of information within the site, ensuring that the visitor knows where they are and also where they should go next from any point on the site.

Site Navigation

Navigation has a number of purposes:

- To present the visitor with the simplest route through the site
- To guide the visitor to those parts of the site that you want them to see
- To enable the visitor to access the required content easily
- To ensure the visitor knows where they are at all times
- To set some context for the current page and topic.

> 'Keep section names easy to understand. Unless you are willing to spend time educating your audience, they may not understand. Try and make it easy to get to all the key areas of the site from any point in the site. Don't try and second-guess where people will want to go – they will surprise you. Give them plenty of options all the time.
>
> Liz Citron
> MD, Arehaus

There is no single perfect method of site navigation, but the best sites offer three alternatives:

- Navigation links
- A search tool
- A site map or site index.

Navigation Links

Clear and consistent navigation buttons (or text links) on each page give the visitor some context (both within and beyond the current section), guiding them to their next click and illustrating the site structure. The BBC (http://www.bbc.co.uk) uses its left-hand navigation column brilliantly, with top-level links combined with links to related information from each

> 'If you really *must* restructure your site so that URLs change, offer some help to people who've got the old ones bookmarked or are following out-of-date links from other pages: tell them whatever you can about the relationship between the old and new site structure to help them find the page they need.'
>
> **Pam Davies**
> **Leeds University Library**

page. Similarly Amazon (http://www.amazon.co.uk) offers consistent links on every page to guide the user to key sections of the site.

Whether text-based or graphical, the links should be explicit and unambiguous. The user should be able to trust that on each page there will be a familiar range of options to guide him or her forwards, backwards or further in to the site.

Search Tools

A search tool is essential for larger sites, but even small sites can benefit from a keyword search facility. The ability to drill down in to the site, searching by keywords, means that a user can access information which matches his or her needs, and not just what has been provided by the site links. Of course, new users may not know what is available and may have no idea what keywords to search on.

Implementing a search tool can provide a technical challenge, depending on the server software used and the arrangement of the content. One simple way out is to use a Web-based solution such as that provided by Atomz.com.

Atomz.com (http://www.atomz.com) provides a Web-based method of creating a site search tool. For sites with up to 500 pages it is entirely free, while larger sites pay a sliding scale of annual fees, with a 2,500-page site costing $600 per year, for example.

By signing up to Atomz.com and entering your web site details, the search tool can be set up for public use in just a few minutes.

Features include:

- indexing of HTML documents, PDF files and text within Flash movies
- configurable results page to integrate seamlessly with your own site's design
- no banner adverts on results, just a discreet 'Powered by Atomz.com' logo
- automatic weekly indexing, or manual initiation on demand
- the ability to search several URLs, and exclude directories as required
- support for many non-Latin character sets
- simple or advanced 'power' search dialogue for your site
- the ability to enter synonyms, phonetic search terms and documents that match specific terms in Atomz.com to help searchers on your site.

Atomz.com simple search dialogue: *Atomz.com power search dialogue:*

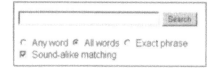   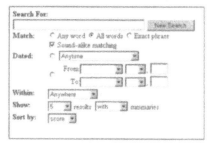

Other providers of Web-based search tools include whatUseek (http://intra.whatuseek.com) and Master.com (http://www.master.com).

Site Map or Index

A site map or directory listing gives the visitor a snapshot of the total information on the site. The British Library site index (http://www.bl.uk) is an elegant example of how a straightforward page listing, colour-coded for each part of the site, provides clear direction and explains the site structure instantly. Similarly the eBay auction site (http://www.ebay.com) has a clear site map that helps users see an enormous amount of information about the services offered, as well as the goods on sale.

The site map may be presented in a graphical format, but a simple file listing (grouped in subject or directory order) is perfectly adequate, and the simpler arrangement will probably be clearer for the user. For small or medium-sized web sites that are not dynamically generated from databases, site-mapping software such as PowerMapper (http://www.electrum.co.uk) can be used to generate a site index automatically, offering a choice of graphical or text versions, with links to each page already created.

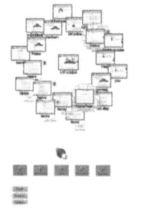

Four site views by PowerMapper 2.0: top, table of contents view; left, cloud view; above, isometric view (thumbnail version); bottom left, 3D view. In all cases the individual pages are clickable links, so your site map or index is created for you.

This sort of tool is ideal for assessing the distribution of content across several directories and for creating checklists of files for updating. It is also useful for understanding the structure of other web sites.

Elements of Content

There are certain obvious expectations from an organisation's web site. It should present the company or organisation to its audience, outline its services or products, and provide a means of making further contact.

This is not always as obvious as it sounds: many web sites do not provide easy access to essential information. How many times have you tried to find a contact telephone number on a web site without success?

The following checklists are for guidance – there are no formal rules of content on the Web, and you may have valid reasons for excluding any of these elements. At one level everything is optional, but remember – it is the user who counts, and it is what he or she is expecting to see that should guide your decisions as to whether or not to include a particular element.

Home Page

- **Logo/name** – it is useful to give the user immediate confirmation that they have reached the right site
- **Location** – it can help to prevent confusion amongst potential customers if you show that your service is limited to geographical territories
- **Contact details** – for a proportion of your visitors, this may all they have come to the site to find
- **Brief outline** – a short tagline summarising your core activity provides further confirmation that the visitor is at the right site
- **Links** – including links to key areas within your site draws the visitor in to read the content or use the service
- **Search option** – to provide further assistance to your visitor, include a search dialogue box on the home page, or at the very least a link to your search tool and site index.

Content Pages

You should consider including these elements on each and every page within the site. Remember that visitors' entry points to your site will differ, depending on whether they have followed a link from another site or found you from a search engine result.

- **Title** – the page title is part of the HTML code, and appears at the top of the browser window. A title is essential for every page as it is stored as the name of a bookmark or favourite and displayed in search engine results – the search engines treat words in the title as having more importance when ranking a page against a searcher's keywords

- **Heading** – the visitor's eye should fall easily on the topic of the page. It could be a graphic or text in a large font or in the tag: the important thing is that it is clear and unambiguous so the visitor knows instantly what the page is about

- **Date** – this can be useful to demonstrate when the page was written, especially if the content is time-sensitive. However, it can also reveal your lack of attention if the date is not changed for a while! Consider omitting this on pages that change rarely

- **Links** – there should be one-click access to your home page, contact details, the top of current section, other pages within the current section, site index and legal statements

- **Search** – enable the visitor to start a new search from anywhere on the site, rather than forcing them to go to a specific page

- **Ownership** – include an e-mail address to respond to or post queries to, perhaps with a statement of ownership or responsibility for the page's content. This is particularly important for sites created by a range of contributors

- **Contact** – this should be more than just an e-mail link. Your address and phone numbers, location map and contact names, departmental contacts and e-mail addresses all ensure that enquiries are directed to the appropriate destination

- **Copyright** – if this is complicated, then place a clear link to a fully detailed copyright page; do the same with a disclaimer if necessary, and privacy and security statements (see Chapter 5 for detailed examples)

- **Feedback** – give users direct contact with web site management to report errors or faults

- **About us** – some elements that are seen on many sites (particularly those belonging to non-commercial, educational and research organisations) are there for purely internal reasons and have little to do with user expectations or customer service. Items such as committee structures, organisation history, minutes of meetings, departmental relationships, constitutions and memoranda can of course be relevant, but should perhaps be placed within a discreet section

- **Help** – provide both on-line assistance and contact details for further information. Possibly also link to live help (see section at end of Chapter 3)
- **FAQ** – a FAQ (frequently asked questions) section can be useful for sites with services that require further explanation. FAQs can either be predicted, or built from actual questions received
- **Orders** or **Customer Service** – commercial sites will also have a link to this area from each page.

To avoid an endless left-hand navigation column, some of the less prominent elements may be placed more discreetly – typically in a small font at the foot of the page. Although they will easily be found and are in a consistent location on the page, they can nevertheless be separated from the more prominent links to core content. These less prominent links might include: home/copyright/disclaimer/privacy/contact/search/site map/about us.

What is the Core Content?

So far in this section you have seen checklists of expected elements, mostly designed to assist visitors on their journey through your web site. The real content, of course, is that which supports your central mission – articles, instructions, publications, news, products and services.

The specific purpose for your site – or a section of it – may be one or more of the following:

- Promote a product or service
- Provide service information
- Collect orders or enquiries
- Provide database access
- Deliver training and support
- Recruit staff
- Host community discussions
  Deliver a product or service
- Offer curriculum support
- Deliver printed materials
- Act as a print depository
- Provide a communications link
- Act as a launch pad to wider resources.

The assumption here is that you already have this content identified, and it is the arrangement, presentation and promotion of it that brings you to this book. But the identification and assessment of appropriate content is as crucial a part of the planning process as the selection of styles, designs and colours.

Throughout the process you should be asking yourself – and your current or potential visitors – what will make the site more useful, informative and comprehensive? What will actually get in the way by confusing the visitor, and what will assist their understanding?

'When redesigning sites, it's hard to create a more logical structure without being influenced by what is already there. Write down every piece of content to be included in the site on a separate Post-It note and stick them all on a noticeboard. Use different colours to delineate types of content, e.g. static, dynamic. Stick them up there in no order at all and just add new ideas for content: after a week or so you'll already have some ideas of how to structure the site. You could do the same thing with a WYSIWYG site editor, but it's better to concentrate on the site structure away from your computer. When I've organised my Post-Its into a logical structure, then I start thinking about actual design.'

Kylie Baxter
School of Law, University of Hull

References and Resources

Site Search Services

Atomz.com (http://www.atomz.com)

Master.com (http://www.master.com)

whatUseek (http://intra.whatuseek.com)

Site Mapping Tools

PowerMapper (http://www.electrum.co.uk)

Site Feature: Content Management

Web site development includes selecting and structuring site content, but managing this crucial element of the site effectively requires a methodical approach to the topic. At the simplest level, 'content' includes everything on the site delivered to the visitor's browser, but 'content management' normally implies that there is a higher level of value to the information – documents, articles and reports, but potentially multimedia, software, news and statistical or financial data. Transactional content – that relating to sales and orders or to database output – is another type of information that requires sophisticated management tools.

Content management is the process of collecting, storing, delivering and monitoring information vital to the organisation. In web site terms, this includes uploading, storing and serving the information to those who need it, but only to those authorised to see it. As a concept, content management is often seen as a technical activity based around intranet, knowledge management or archive systems and processes, but it can also encompass the whole life-cycle of information from creation to deletion.

For the purposes of this book, content management is approached from a web site manager's perspective. This involves the allocation of staff time to the creation or selection of appropriate information, the conversion of that information to a format that can be delivered over a net-

> 'A content management system is a concept not a product. No off-the-shelf product will cover all your needs, so think about buying and building.'
>
> **Mike Lowndes**
> **Web Manager, Natural History Museum**

work when requested by the user, and a series of limitations to ensure that documents are secure, up-to-date, searchable, attributable and accessible.

Manual solutions – involving individuals converting, naming and linking documents through the web site – are inevitably time-consuming, so automated solutions have been developed to alleviate the effort required to deliver the information on demand.

Key requirements of a content management system include the following:

- **Web facilitation** – templates, wizards or conversion tools to enable non-experts to deposit documents into a retrieval system. This could be as simple as a directory into which Word documents are filed, with the filenames listed as the directory home page; or it could be a sophisticated document-delivery system with browser plug-ins that convert the documents as they are called up by users, so that they can be viewed in the browser.

- **Format management** – documents from legacy collections (those not created specifically for the current system) need to be organised by format for easy management, and converted into suitable delivery and viewing formats (perhaps HTML or PDF, or TIFF images for scanned documents). These formats then allow the documents to be shared with third parties if that is required. Data may also be in audio or video formats, spreadsheets or databases. An advanced content management system will be able to deliver all of these files through the browser window – with the appropriate plug-ins where necessary (Acrobat, Flash, QuickTime, RealPlayer, etc.).

- **Revision tracking** – file naming and dating protocols (standards imposed upon or agreed by the organisation) should ensure that document versions can be identified. This is essential if a series of rewritten documents is involved, such as financial regulations or contracts where access to superseded versions may be required. The identity of the author, and of those who update and revise the document, should be available for security, audit and referencing purposes.

- **Indexing, searching and retrieval** – in order to be useful and usable, the data has to be easily accessible. This implies some form of cataloguing and classification, and will usually depend on the author rigorously following the naming protocols (and perhaps the addition of other information such as keywords, subject classification, date of publication, etc.).

- **Access management** – while the entire system might be protected from external access by firewall software or simple password security, internally to the organisation there will be further levels of access control. Management, financial and marketing information will carry different levels of restriction, depending on the nature of the information itself and on the structure of the organisation.

An advanced knowledge-based organisation may have all staff involved in the development and management of the content management system – in other organisations there may be a core team to whom documents are delivered for conversion, classification and cataloguing.

The Microsoft web site provides a white paper on content management systems that describes the process and requirements of an effective content management system: http://www.microsoft.com/technet/ecommerce/contmgt.asp

Some Example Content Management System Products

Red Snapper (http://www.redsnapper.net)
SDLWebFlow (http://www.sdlintl.com)
Vignette (http://www.vignette.co.uk)
Kosmos (http://www.tss.ie)

Case Studies 1

EARL

Countrybookshop.co.uk

EEVL

Cambridge University Press

Institute of Actuaries

The case studies in this book are from distinctive web sites in a range of sectors, and yet there are several recurring themes – the need to be in continual development, the importance of an understanding of the site's audience and their expectations, and the importance of reliability and accessibility. The case studies in this first group are all broadly from the information sector, including publishers and booksellers, specialist information resources and membership organisations providing educational and professional services. Several have members and subscribers, while some know them as customers or students, but the shared commitment to delivering a reliable, usable and accessible service is evident. Practical marketing activities and the struggle to establish a workable database solution also feature in several of these studies.

Links to the web sites and services featured in the case studies and throughout this book can be found on the supporting web site, http://www.webtipsandtricks.co.uk

EARL (Electronic Access to Resources in Libraries)

(http://www.earl.org.uk)

The networking of public libraries – indeed, the creation of a people's network of information access – is high on the agenda of the UK government. Since 1995, through the EARL Consortium for Public Library Networking, public libraries have been working collaboratively with strategic partners from government, universities, museums, archives and the private sector to promote the creation of networked, web-based services at the national level. Through its web site, EARL (Electronic Access to Resources in Libraries) has launched a series of demonstrator services that have developed into fully fledged national services. These include 'Ask a Librarian', which is an award-winning on-line enquiry service; 'Familia', a national database of family and local history information; and 'Euroguide', a subject gateway to web sites containing information on the European Union. Other key features are the information portal EARL*web*, various discussion lists and the EARL newsletter.

Frames: no	JavaScript: yes	Java: no
Flash: yes	Audio/video: no	Animation: no
HTML editor: Allaire HomeSite 4.5 (30 percent), Microsoft FrontPage 98 (10 percent), manual coding (60 percent)		
Database: Microsoft Access (local database), Perl CGI script (web databases)		
FTP: WS_FTP 95 Pro	Graphics: Adobe Photoshop	
Server software: UNIX		
Team: three people		
Design: in-house		
History: launched in 1995; redesigned August 2000		
Monthly page views: 120,000		
Site size: 92 mb		
Usability: optimised for maximum accessibility with all browsers		

By Linda Berube (Development and UKEL Co-ordinator) and Sally Chambers (Liaison Officer & Ask a Librarian Coordinator), with Godfrey Oswald (Information Officer & Website Developer)

Background

An important function of the site, especially during the early days of the consortium, was to serve as an exemplar upon which public libraries could base their own sites. In keeping with this function, the site, a series of flat HTML pages constructed without the use of an HTML editor, complies with the guidelines of the W3C (World Wide Web Consortium, http://www.w3.org) and Bobby (http://www.cast.org/bobby). In addition to providing information and demonstrator services, EARL continues to design and maintain sites for libraries and non-profit and government agencies.

Audience: Who is the Web Site For?

As with any consortium the most important element is the partners, and the central web site is therefore targeted towards those partners. Because the EARL consortium consists of over 75 percent of UK public library authorities, the needs and concerns of public libraries are central to the organisation and content of the web site. In turn, the needs of library users are the main concern of the public libraries. This range of interests has been addressed in the design of the EARL web site. Although the public library users and the libraries that service them are the main target audience of the EARL web site, it is hoped that the site will also satisfy other groups that fall outside this category.

How the Site was Built

As the EARL Consortium is a national grouping of public library authorities it was of paramount importance that there was good communication between the partners. Because of the diverse geographical locations, and the emphasis placed on the inclusion of Wales, Scotland and Northern Ireland in the work of EARL, a central communication tool was necessary; and as the consortium is focused on the networking of public libraries, a web-based dissemination tool seemed ideal. The importance of the EARL web site was therefore established right from the outset.

Because the EARL web site had to address the needs of a diverse audience, it was originally based on a three-strand content structure:

- information about EARL
- A–Z listing of EARL partners
- EARL*web* (an information portal of resources relevant to UK public library users).

Although this structure is still inherent in the current web site, as the work of the EARL Consortium has diversified the web site has expanded.

Originally each partner was allowed up to 20 mb of space on the EARL server for information about their library service. These partner web pages were originally created by EARL's first information officer, but the work was later contracted out to Input Output, who designed a standardised format for the public library partners. These pages, which are centrally collected in an A–Z list on the EARL web site (http://www.earl.org.uk/partners/), are still a feature of the present web site, although quite a few authorities are now designing and maintaining their sites on their own servers.

EARLweb
At EARL's inception the amount of networked information that was directly relevant to the diverse needs of the public library user community in the UK was very small. Although structured sets of networked information were available for other user groups, for example the UK higher education community, there was a need for a similar data set for public libraries. Thus EARL*web* (http://www.earl.org.uk/earlweb/) was born.

EARL*web*, originally conceived by an independent consultant, was constructed as a demonstrator gateway to major networked services in key subjects, as a web training tool for public librarians and as a suitable medium to develop shared resources with national, regional and local information. In 1997 consultants from the library field developed EARL*web* into a fully fledged national service. It is subdivided into eight sections:

- The Global Library
- Imagination and memory
- Lifelong learning
- The online enquiry desk
- Science and technology
- Business intelligence
- The citizen in society
- The Public Librarian.

Discussion Lists
To foster collaboration between EARL partners, public librarians and other interested parties, and to provide a current awareness service, EARL runs 15 electronic discussion lists. These range from a general discussion list for EARL partners, through a special list for library and information students with an interest in public library networking issues, to more specific subject-based lists for members and contributors

to the different task groups that the consortium maintains. EARL is also involved in several research and development projects, which have discussion lists to aid efficient dissemination of information. Although these projects are not listed on the EARL web site, they are still part of the overall picture. The electronic discussion lists were set up by independent consultants, who used Majordomo (http://www. greatcircle.com/ majordomo/) for list management. Nowadays the EARL Information Officer acts as the list owner for all the EARL electronic discussion lists. As all the lists are closed, to avoid members receiving spam or junk mail, it is part of the Information Officer's job to approve subscriptions to the list. An acceptable use policy for the discussion lists has recently been formulated (http://www.earl.org.uk/lists/policy.html).

Issues, Solutions and Outcomes

EARL: A New Look
In the summer of 1999 the EARL web site underwent its first major revision. More constant and consistent updating and revision of the site is now part of our permanent policy. The major areas addressed were design, accessibility, navigation and functionality.

The Issues
Design, Accessibility, Navigation and Functionality
The basic site layout and graphic design had not been changed for approximately four years. The site therefore had a somewhat dated appearance, and it was felt that the colour scheme was rather dark. In the redesign we were looking for something cleaner, with a lighter (preferably white) background colour to improve accessibility. The layout of the old front page prevented the addition of material to alert users to news about the consortium or new features on the site, and the primary search method was through a tool bar, which was particularly restrictive because it was difficult to add links to new categories of

The front page of the old EARL web site.

material. A revision was vital, not only because of the demand for the new, different and most current on the Web, but also because a primary function of the site is to serve as a model for good practice in public library web site design.

The Solutions

Design and Functionality

Because the site is informational in nature, and representative of a national organisation, we wanted the new site to be straightforward and not commercial in its presentation. We decided not to use frames or an excess of JavaScript for accessibility reasons. In keeping with a somewhat serious, professional appearance, we also avoided too many graphics, especially of the animated variety.

The new colour scheme marked a radical departure from the dark and sombre background of the previous years, and with the white background we were also able to give greater prominence to our logo.

The front page was restructured to include a continually updated news section on one half of the page. Because EARL*web* was the only service specifically identified on the old search tool bar it received what might be considered a disproportionate amount of visits, apparently at the expense of the other services. We therefore eliminated EARL*web* from the current tool bar and included it in the list of other services in the drop-down menu and in the rotating list of logos for services on the other half of the front page. As of October 2000 we are still in the process of redesigning these logos. In the meantime we are experimenting with banners, representing each of the services, appearing randomly on each page. It is through the banners, as well as the logos, that we are able to include more colourful and eye-catching elements on the page, and perhaps generate more interest in the services themselves. We are also exploring banner exchange as a way of increasing interest in the services.

Navigation

The pages on the EARL web site have been redesigned to include text navigation sections running along the top and bottom of each page. An extensive text index and a search facility are also available to aid navigation. Most pages have a section, running down the left, which summarises what the user can expect to find on that page.

Clicking on the EARL logo at the top of each page takes the user back to the EARL home page. JavaScript navigation menus have been included in some areas of the site, but all pages are accessible to those using older or non-JavaScript-enabled web browsers. User feedback should be easier because we have included a feedback form on the site, and made our contact details more easily accessible. We didn't eliminate the tool bar entirely, but instead increased the navigation options using a drop-down menu that would allow new categories to be added, and included a search option for the site.

Accessibility and Compatibility

We tested the new EARL web site across a wide range of browsers. It is still difficult to ensure complete compatibility, especially when using cascading style sheets (CSS) to format the textual information within each page. Only browsers from version 4 upwards support CSS formatting; older browsers will still display the text but will not format it in the style that is defined in the style sheet. JavaScript has been used on only a small number of pages that do not provide core functionality and is hidden from incompatible web browsers.

Critique of Solutions: What We Have Learned

Complete satisfaction with the design of a web site is rare. So although we find the new site much more flexible in terms of updating, and have had nothing but positive feedback on the initial redesign, we can't help but look towards the next revision. For instance, we made every attempt to improve navigability on the site, but are just in the preparatory stages of the ultimate in navigability: the database. This development will have its greatest effect on EARL*web*, which for now remains as flat HTML pages with hypertext links.

We are always on the lookout for the newest technologies that offer the latest in accessibility and navigation. For instance, it is possible that we will use more DHTML (dynamic HTML) as more browsers become able to handle it. Because we regularly review the Internet media for new technologies we are able to consistently assess our site against published examples of best practice. We also rely on Jacob Neilson's Useit site (http://www.useit.com) and the W3C site (http://www.w3c.org) for guidance.

We are looking to increase the presence of all our home country partners on the site. Currently, in the main A–Z listing of EARL partners (http://www.earl.org.uk/partners/), Scottish and Welsh partners are highlighted with the use of Welsh dragon and Scottish thistle emblems. We hope to extend this visual representative to Northern Ireland partners shortly. Through liaison with the Cymru (Welsh language) task group we have almost completed a Welsh language version of 'Ask a Librarian', which will be staffed entirely by Welsh EARL partners. Key areas of the web site and the EARL services are also being translated into Welsh, and we are identifying and highlighting Internet resources that relate specifically to Welsh-speaking citizens.

Web sites traditionally have a short shelf life. As mentioned previously, we have now incorporated a regular revision schedule (probably every two years or less) into our web development cycle. We are currently developing a much wider-ranging portal, the UK Electronic Library; this will not only incorporate EARL*web* and the current services, but also include a database of specialised book collections around the country as well as an international on-line enquiry service.

http://www.earl.org.uk

@arl
The Consortium for Public Library Networking

Countrybookshop.co.uk

(http://www.countrybookshop.co.uk)

Countrybookshop.co.uk is now firmly established as the on-line/ WAP option for readers who wish to make their book purchases from the local alternative to the global on-line bookstores.

For the past 13 years we have been selling books from an old railway station in the Peak National Park. Our web site was set up in-house in 1997 to complement the established bricks-and-mortar shop, and in March 1999 we relaunched it with the ability to sell every title in print in the UK – more than one million titles.

We receive over 1.3 million page views per month and countrybookshop.co.uk is now the UK's second most popular bookselling site and its number one dedicated on-line bookshop. We were ranked number 41 in *The Sunday Times* e-League – European Top 100 Internet Ventures (2 July 2000), and recently achieved second place in the DTI ISI/InterForum East Midlands Region E-Commerce Awards.

By Geraldine Rose and Sridhar Gowda
(Directors, countrybookshop.co.uk)

Frames: no	JavaScript: on occasion	Java: on occasion
Flash: a little	Audio/video: no	Animation: no
HTML editor: PFE (Programmer's File Editor), Dreamweaver		
Database: MySQL		
FTP: FTP Voyager	Graphics: Photoshop	
Server software: Linux, Apache		
Team: six people		
Design: outsourced		
History: launched August 1997		
Monthly page views: 1.3 million		
Usability: optimised for all browsers		

Background

Prior to 1997 Country Bookshop was an independent bricks-and-mortar bookseller for the local community and visitors to the Peak National

Park. We offered a broad selection of books in nearly every genre, including local books, and had a particularly large selection for children and young adults. We also provided a book-ordering facility, bargain books, a friendly shopping atmosphere and literary events, including an annual poetry competition for children. In addition, we worked on literary projects with schools and libraries. The bookshop continued to grow even though many other independents were closing at the time with the aggressive expansion of the chain booksellers.

In 1997 we realised that another medium presented itself for the promotion and sales of books – the World Wide Web. We wanted to serve our local customers better by offering our services through this medium, and also hoped to promote our shop. Our site was first launched with just a selection of titles, but we quickly realised that on-line customers required full access to the entire database of books in print and so we decided to re-launch the site with every UK title in print.

As we are a small, independent bookseller, the site had to be built in the most cost-effective way that would be sustainable and scalable for future growth. After extensive research, and with the experience gained from running the site for a year, we decided to go for the open-source solution. Eric Raymond's paper 'The Cathedral and the Bazaar' (first given as a paper at the 1997 Linux Kongress, and published in 1999 by O'Reilly), the O'Reilly web site (http://www.oreilly.com) and the growing user-base of the Linux community strengthened our belief in the open-source community. We chose the Linux operating system, Apache web server and MySQL database, all of which have served us well. Perl and PHP were used as our programming languages. The site was built in-house to integrate the understanding of bookselling and customer needs, and was re-launched in March 1999 with over one million titles.

Once the site was built came the task of promoting it alongside the big players with their huge marketing budgets. We have grown organically to become the number one dedicated on-line bookshop and the second most popular on-line site selling books in the UK (Alexa statistics), without any external investment. We feel we have competed effectively without any marketing spend in the following ways.

Web Usability

We concentrated on making our site user-friendly, clean and easily navigable. We developed a quick-and-easy search facility that can be used to search by title, author or ISBN, and an advanced search facility that uses publisher, category or series, and can be sorted by title, author, publisher or price. We also list our books in topic categories in case customers are unsure of the exact title. We ensured that our site was compatible with various current browsers, such as Internet Explorer and Netscape, on PC and Linux platforms, etc., and also that it worked with previous versions. We focused on minimising the load time by avoiding the use of unnecessary graphics, and believe that it's good practice to double-check spelling and ensure that there are no dead links. To appreciate the end-users' perspective we recommend Jacob Nielsen's book *Designing Web Usability*, and his site Useit.com.

User Feedback

From the very beginning we have listened to our customers' feedback. We use BizRate.com, a third party validation service which enables customers to check the rating applied to our site by other customers and give feedback on the service provided by countrybookshop.co.uk (no other online bookshop does this), so making our site transparent. So far we have been rated by over 25,000 customers, who are asked to give their feedback on the following criteria: ease of ordering, product selection, product information, price, web site performance, on-time delivery, product representation, customer support, order tracking and shipping and handling.

We listen to what our customers are saying about our site, and use this direct feedback to improve the quality of our service.

Search Engines and Web Directories

We registered our site with many web directories such as Yahoo, Netscape, etc. (sites like !Register-it! allow you to register with several search engines in one go). Before submitting your site it's important to check your tags to ensure that the web pages are set up to be indexed correctly by search engines and directories. Web Site Garage gives a free report on your site, with recommendations for improving or fixing tags, browser compatibility, load time, dead links, spelling and HTML coding. Our site was also registered with shopping directories like Shopsmart, with trade associations and regional web sites, and with pay-per-click search engines such as GoTo, godado.com, etc. The advantage of the pay-per-click search engines is that you can get your site registered immediately, and be on the top of the listing for the keywords that you have bought. (We bought 'Harry Potter' as a keyword for a penny at GoTo.) PayPerClickSearchEngines.com lists more than 40 search engines that sell keywords.

Alexa, the web navigation tool, is very useful for finding directories, thus providing extra sites to submit to. It is also useful for finding the popularity of the site to which you are submitting. Sites that link to your site can be found by typing link:yourdomainname in the search box at AltaVista. The same facility can also be used to find links to sites with keywords that are suitable for your site. This is done by performing a link check for competing sites (type link:competingdomainname in the

AltaVista search box) and using View/Source in the browser to see what keywords appear to be useful.

Customer Service

We realise that it is still important to retain the human touch and therefore we provide a freephone number on every page of our web site. Our customer support personnel are available seven days a week, and we also provide an on-line order tracking facility. We offer a returns facility with clear information and a freepost address. Customers can open an account with us, leaving their address and payment details so that they do not have to be re-entered on subsequent visits.

The site is hosted on a secure server so that customers' information and payment details are secure. The majority of banks and card issuers will cover any unauthorised use of credit cards or limit the customer's liability to £50; we offer to cover this liability. We offer competitive postal rates, discount many of our titles and have a price promise which guarantees that we will meet the price of any other on-line bookshop. We accept payment by cheque and postal order, as well as credit card, to make life easier for our customers.

We have worked with web currency company Beenz since their launch and now also deal with Ycreds, which is a payment system for customers under 18 years of age who have no access to credit cards. We are the only on-line bookshop to offer this payment system.

To increase consumer confidence we registered with the Which? Web Trader Scheme and with ePublicEye, who act as consumer watchdogs. We value our customers' privacy and we have a clearly defined privacy policy that is posted on our site.

Content, Interactivity and Additional Services

We list all the book award winners (e.g. Booker Prize, Whitbread Awards, Carnegie, etc.) for the current and previous years on our site, publish author interviews (some also in audio format), list the current best-sellers in different categories, and give details of nationwide author events.

Our literary quiz has become one of the most popular on-line quizzes, helping to make the site 'sticky', and customers have helped us by providing lots of questions. The competitions are held regularly and customers have the opportunity to win books.

Some titles ordered are unfortunately out of print, and as we wish to offer our customers a complete service in books we also provide an out-of-print service whereby an out-of-print dealers network is used to source the books requested. We also list over a thousand remaindered and promotional books that are discounted by up to 85 percent.

Affiliates

Our affiliate programme has been very successful, and brings in a significant proportion of our orders. We offer up to 10 percent commission on the sales coming through our affiliate sites. Our affiliates include Egg, btspree.com, bluecarrots, BT OpenWorld, dooyoo, Deal-Time, etc. (We now have 55,150 affiliates linked to our site). Our affiliate program was submitted to various affiliate directories such as Refer-it and AssociatePrograms.com.

When our affiliates have run promotions to their subscribers, using e-mails, newsletters or advertising, we have co-operated by supplying content and promotions with links to our site to attract (and hopefully retain) new customers.

We are also the mail-order supplier to *Gardening Which?* magazine subscribers.

Revolution and *New Media Magazine* are useful resources for finding up-and-coming new players as potential partners and associates, and e-mail alerts from Silicon.com and netimperative.com are also useful sources of information on e-commerce trends and marketing developments.

Media Coverage and Awards

We do not miss an opportunity to promote our site, so we make submissions for awards and have often been pleasantly surprised to find that we win these awards. For example, we gained second place in the DTI ISI/InterForum East Midlands Region E-Commerce Awards; we were number 41 in *The Sunday Times* e-League – European Top 100 Internet Ventures; and Geraldine Rose (our co-founder) was placed in the top five of the Top 100 Future Entrepreneurs by *Enterprise Magazine,* KPMG and the London Business School.

From the outset we have received good press on the look and feel of our site from several new media magazines. We send out regular targeted press releases to the local press, new media magazines, trade press and the national press, and when possible speak on local radio and give TV interviews.

Exhibitions, Conferences and Networking

We exhibit at various trade fairs, including the BBC Tomorrows' World Exhibition, Internet World 2000, E-Business 2000, Internet Business 2000, and at local Chamber of Commerce and Business Link exhibitions in order to publicise our site and meet our customers in person. We have written articles, given talks and made presentations for the bookselling press, publishers, new media seminars, etc., on the subject of on-line bookselling and new media.

We attend various conferences and new media gatherings, which are useful for networking opportunities.

New Technology

We embrace new technology as it presents itself: for example, the site recently became WAP-enabled in preparation for the time when WAP (wireless application protocol) becomes popular. Because we are the first UK bookseller to move in this direction it has allowed us to make alliances with companies such as Iobox, Snaz, etc.

Conclusion

We are pleased with what we have achieved so far. It would have been easier and more expeditious to reach our target with financial backing from the beginning, but in retrospect maybe the lack of external investment has resulted in a site that is unique in many ways and has also produced a viable business model, which is not so common in the dotcom world.

We were pleasantly surprised to find that we could grow so rapidly in this organic way, and over the eighteen months or so since the re-launch of our site to sell every book in print our on-line sales have increased so that they now far outstrip our retail shop sales.

Obviously we looked at our on-line competitors, and in the beginning had no thought of ever competing with the big players in our sector with their huge financial backing. However, we found that we quickly overtook many sites and finally, in September 2000, overtook all but one UK book-selling site in popularity – and still our sales continue to grow.

We are now frequently asked to develop and provide new media solutions for other companies and so we have created another venture, Inamaste (http://www.inamaste.com), to fulfil this need. This seems to be another rapidly growing area of our business, and we are finding it interesting to use our new media expertise and business experience to offer cost-effective solutions for sustainable competitive advantage.

References and Resources

Web sites and services cited in the text above (in order of appearance):

Alexa (http://www.alexaresearch.com)
>Traffic ratings of top 50 sites in 30 countries, derived from users of Alexa, a free downloadable web navigation and search tool

BizRate.com (http://www.bizrate.com)

Comparison shopping service that ranks on-line stores according to ratings provided by customers

!Register-It! (http://www.register-it.com)
Free service from Netscape enabling submission of your site's URL to 12 leading search engines

Web Site Garage (http://www.websitegarage.com)
Another Netscape-owned service that tests your page for spelling, HTML errors, link errors, loading speeds, image file sizes, etc.

ShopSmart (http://uk.shopsmart.com)
On-line shopping directory listing 1,000 UK stores with ratings based on ease of use, quality and service

GoTo (http://www.goto.com)
A pay-per-click search engine where advertisers bid for specific keywords, only paying on click-throughs

godado.com (http://www.godado.tv)
European-specific pay-per-click search engine, charging for results placement click-throughs

PayPerClickSearchEngines.com (http://www.payperclicksearchengines.com)
Information site that lists, reviews and compares pay-per-click search engines such as GoTo and godado.com

AltaVista (http://www.altavista.com)
Search engine – type link:yourdomainname to show up all links to your site, or use to check links to competitors for possible link requests

Beenz (http://www.beenz.com)
A virtual currency earned as loyalty points from buying, searching or surfing on web sites, redeemable in exchange for purchases

yCreds (http://www.ycreds.co.uk)
An alternative to credit cards, yCreds (or SmartCreds) are on-line vouchers aimed at children and young adults, with accounts that can be topped-up and used to make on-line purchases

Which? Web Trader Scheme (http://www.which.net/webtrader/)
Acceptance on this scheme permits use of a logo to show that you undertake to abide by the Which? code of conduct in dealing with customers on-line

ePublicEye (http://www.epubliceye.com)
A shopping directory that acts as 'an independent third party that allows consumers to rate e-business for reliability, privacy and customer satisfaction'

Egg (http://www.egg.com)
Part of the Prudential banking group, Egg offers credit cards and other financial services as well as shopping through its web site; card holders can earn loyalty points

btspree.com (http://www.btspree.com)
On-line shopping directory from BT, offering price comparisons as well as shopping guides and added-value information

BT OpenWorld (http://www.btopenworld.com)
BT's new international mass market ISP, an Internet business focusing on broadband and mobile services

DealTime (http://www.dealtime.co.uk)
Another free on-line shopping comparison site, which searches out bargains and sends e-mail updates

dooyoo (http://www.dooyoo.co.uk)
A platform for consumer opinions; visitors can share their views of products and services and are paid with 'dooyoo miles'

Refer-it (http://www.refer-it.com)
A directory of 3,000+ affiliate and referral programs on the Internet, with programs rated by revenue, clarity and content

AssociatePrograms.com (http://www.associateprograms.com)
Another directory of 3,000+ affiliate programs searchable by payment type, theme or sector with tips on making affiliate programs pay

EEVL (Edinburgh Engineering Virtual Library)

New: The Internet Aviator

(http://www.eevl.ac.uk)

EEVL – the Edinburgh Engineering Virtual Library – is a portal to engineering information on the Internet. Based at Heriot-Watt University Library in Edinburgh, and with partners at a number of universities and professional institutions in the UK, EEVL was created to provide access to quality engineering information on the Internet.

It was originally one of a number of projects funded by the higher education funding councils via the Joint Information Systems Committee (JISC) as part of the Electronic Libraries Programme (eLib), and is now part of the Resource Discovery Network (RDN). The project began in August 1995, went live as a service in September 1996, and, while remaining true to the original objective, has developed significantly in the years since.

By Linda Kerr (EEVL Coordinator) and Roddy MacLeod (EEVL Manager)

Frames: no	JavaScript: yes	Java: yes
Flash: no	Audio/video: no	Animation: no
HTML editor: Dreamweaver 2.0		
Database: written in Java		FTP: WS_FTP
Graphics: Adobe ImageStyler, Macromedia Fireworks, Paint Shop Pro		
Server software: Apache		
Team: five people		
Design: in-house		
History: re-launched November 1999		
Monthly traffic: 190,000 page views, 30,000 visitors		
Site size: 10 gb		
Usability: not optimised for specific browsers		

EEVL is a true child of Internet culture, and was developed to solve the problem of locating quality engineering information for academics, students and researchers in higher education in the UK. Although it is a service that by its very nature can only exist on the Internet, traditional library skills are used throughout the service to select, catalogue and index quality web sites. The web sites are reviewed and evaluated by a team of information experts based at UK universities, who are in touch with end-user needs and who also come across relevant web sites in the course of their day-to-day jobs.

When EEVL went live the main service was a database of descriptions and links to 1,300 web sites ('resources'). The database was both browsable by subject and searchable by keyword. There are now nearly 6,000 sites in the database, representing over 150 different subject areas in engineering, and covering all the major academic sites in the world, as well as journals, institutions, leading engineering software, collections of research papers, companies, courseware and training materials and other relevant information.

In subsequent years a number of additional services have been added. These include full-text search engines, which search only the quality web sites listed in the catalogue, bibliographic databases, an on-line tutorial, a contacts database, lists of the most frequently accessed sites, and sets of pages providing links to such things as other engineering guides and current awareness services. EEVL has received a number of awards, has registered over four million page views, and since April 2000 has provided the top-level WWW Virtual Library for engineering.

Background to the Site Design

There is no such thing as a perfectly designed web site. The design of most sites ends up being a compromise between the aims and creativity of the owner(s) and the needs of the potential visitors, compounded by restrictions placed on the process through the need to present the content in a logical way. The EEVL web site is no different from most others in this respect, except that because of the nature of its intended audience there were, perhaps, more limitations on the extent of its design than there might have been had it been aimed at the general public or solely at the commercial sector.

The primary target audience of EEVL is the academic sector, in particular those students, staff and researchers who are looking for quality information in all engineering disciplines. However, a tool such as EEVL is also of use to the commercial world, and EEVL has always tried to nurture its ties with this sector. A fair proportion of sites included in EEVL's catalogue are, in fact, company web sites, and such is the nature of the subject that there are close ties between engineering academics and practising engineers. Within academia there are both cultural and practical reasons why 'fancy' web sites are not popular. Within the various engineering industries there might almost be said to be a practical or non-frivolous culture. To accommodate these audiences a prerequisite of the EEVL site design was that its structure and style would deliberately be kept simple, with minimal use of graphics. Other important points in the pre-design brief were that the site should be easy to use, its purpose should be apparent from its design, and special software or plug-ins such as Flash or Shockwave should not be required, as it could not be assumed that these would be available to the target audience, many of whom access the Internet via internal networks using only limited software.

Issues

The current site design, which has been live since November 1999, is the fourth version of the EEVL site. The very first one consisted of simple text links on a white background, a rather crude 'EEVL eye' logo, and a search box, all of which were left-justified. Such was the culture of simplicity, that during the design of the second version heated discussions took place as to whether or not any text should be centred! In the third version the original white background was replaced by yellow, and although the site was slightly more graphics-intensive it kept many of the features of the original and was rather verbose. As EEVL continued to add different services, notably targeted full-text search engines and three bibliographic databases, the site began to look overcrowded. A user evaluation survey in 1998 indicated that users found the range of search services confusing and the purpose of the site not obvious from its design. Three of the search engines were subsequently combined into a meta search engine (with the separate search engines still available at other parts of the site), and this was extremely well received by users, but there were still several other seemingly disparate services that needed to be tied together in a coherent way.

The current site design was influenced by a number of factors. The need to integrate various different services has already been mentioned, and the pre-design brief specified that these should be presented in a coherent way, without the need for lengthy text descriptions. The expectations of an increasingly sophisticated user group and the influence of commercial portals were also relevant. The starting point for the design was the idea of a Yahoo-style portal; this was seen as a format which would be familiar to users but fit EEVL's remit and be flexible enough to encompass the range of services on offer. Although we wanted to retain a reasonably serious look and feel, we didn't want EEVL to appear to be simply another academic site, and several trade journal sites were also examined for ideas.

Design Process

A small design team consisting of people working on the EEVL service was formed. Although none of the team members were professional designers, all had extensive Internet experience. This team further developed the design brief, and drafted an initial storyboard for the new web site.

The main points in the final brief were:

- Structure and style should be simple
- The site should be easily navigable
- The site should be easy to use
- The purpose of the site should be obvious from its design
- Graphics should be kept to a minimum, and reused throughout the site
- Special software should not be required
- Frames should not be used
- No log-in or registration should be required
- The catalogue should be the main feature
- A search box should feature on the home page
- The number of 'clicks' needed to retrieve information should be kept to a minimum
- The various services should be integrated as far as possible
- The site should not look overly academic
- The site should be easily manageable
- The site should be expandable
- In-context help pages should be available from all pages
- Feedback should be possible from all pages
- The need for scrolling to reveal features should be kept to a minimum
- Fonts should be uniform throughout
- Funders' logos should be featured
- Space should be provided for a small number of banner adverts
- The site should feature a small number of key awards won by the service.

The design process identified three areas for consideration: look-and-feel, site architecture and content. In addition to the Yahoo-style search box and browse headings, current and planned services were listed and grouped by function. Headings chosen for these, after a great deal of discussion over wording, were 'more services' and 'hot links'. Standard headings for the navigation bar were agreed, and extra links associated with the catalogue were identified.

Solutions

Because the team wanted to keep control over the design process, and in order to reduce the cost of the exercise, it was decided to employ a research student with web design experience to work on the project in-

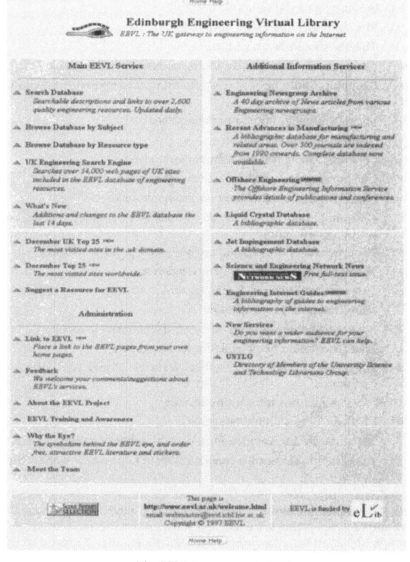

The EEVL home page in 1998.

The EEVL home page in 2000.

house, rather than hand the brief over to a web design company. As well as implementing the design brief the researcher also acted as a catalyst in discussions among the design team. As there were limited funds to pay for subsequent updates to the web site it was essential that the permanent in-house staff could undertake day-to-day editing, and the research student worked closely with them, providing training in the use of relevant software.

Software was purchased in consultation with the researcher. After some discussion it was decided to use Macromedia Dreamweaver 2 to develop the site and create the web pages, and Paint Shop Pro and Adobe ImageStyler to produce the graphics. In addition the researcher used his own copy of Fireworks to produce some of the graphics. A very tight schedule for the production of the site resulted from the desire to feature the new design at a large corporate event.

The outcome was a reasonably coherent design featuring, at the top of the home page, the EEVL logo – a graphic of the 'EEVL eye' combined with the site's name and a very brief description. Underneath this are text, features and a search box divided into tables of two-thirds and one-third width. At the bottom of the page the text-based links are repeated, and small graphics link to the service's funders and to prestigious awards.

Critique

The main lesson learnt from the design process was that the time needed to produce a professional-looking web site should not be underestimated. Deadlines are a necessary evil, and may also encourage completion, but overly tight schedules may mean compromises that cause future complications. In the event there was little time to test the new interface before the service went live, and some adjustments were made after the new design was released. Although the design team was very satisfied with the work of the external researcher, it has not been easy to contact him for additional consultancy work, which would (presumably) not have been the case with a professional agency.

There have been problems in updating the site. Some incompatibilities between web editors meant that pages that included forms could not be edited using Dreamweaver 2, or the forms would mysteriously refuse to work. This problem was eventually sorted out, but in the intervening time all the pages with forms, linked by a Dreamweaver 2 template, were disengaged from the template and edited using Notepad. It has otherwise been relatively straightforward to update the site, although a decision has been made to use Dreamweaver for its original purpose – site management – and purchase a more basic editor for day-to-day updates (HomeSite is under consideration). Because staff will have only a limited amount of time available to spend on the web site it is essential that commitments are not made to labour-intensive new services (e.g. news or current awareness services) without a realistic estimate of the time involved keeping them current and relevant. However, by far the largest maintenance element is the catalogue. Link-checking software is run every month, and this tests all the links to sites listed in the catalogue. Around three hundred 'problem' links are reported each month, and require attention, but in practice a smaller number of sites are actually no longer available. It requires about three days work each month to ensure that all sites referenced in the EEVL catalogue are up-to-date. The descriptions of the web sites also need to be checked on a regular basis – a mammoth task that is only now being implemented in a systematic manner. As the web becomes more a part of our daily lives web sites may be less likely to disappear, but their content will continue to change regularly. No technological solution has been found to this maintenance problem, and it may need to be resolved by making the site descriptions less detailed and less specific.

No formal evaluation of the new site has been made, but informal feedback has indicated that the redesign has not only been appreciated, but has made the site much easier to use than previously. Usage of the site increased dramatically at the time of its launch, and has continued to grow, but many other factors, such as an extensive marketing programme, have undoubtedly also had an impact. The new design was revealed at the launch of the RDN in November 1999, and a press release was sent to various e-mail lists and a number of print publications. A certain amount of press coverage was received, notably in *Industrial Technology,* which is one of the most popular engineering trade journals, and *Information World Review.*

Web site designs are ephemeral. Services such as EEVL constantly evolve and develop, and even within a year of the launch there are signs of a need to review the design to take into account service changes and ever-emerging developments in Web technology. As a result, the estimated life of the current design is unlikely to extend beyond about 18 months.

Cambridge University Press

(http://uk.cambridge.org)

Cambridge University Press is the printing and publishing house of the University of Cambridge. It is an integral part of the University and has similar charitable objectives in advancing knowledge, education, learning and research. For centuries the Press has extended the research and teaching activities of the University by making available worldwide, through its printing and publishing, a remarkable range of academic and educational books, journals, examination papers and Bibles.

By Ivan Salcedo (Web Marketing Manager, Cambridge University Press)

Frames: no	JavaScript: yes	Java: no
Flash: some	Audio/video: no	Animation: yes
HTML editor: Dreamweaver 3.0		
Database: Oracle 7/8I (catalogue); SQL Server 6.5 (Cambridge International Dictionaries) FTP: n/a		
Graphics: Fireworks 3.0, Photoshop 5.5	Server software: NT 4.0 SP6, IIS 4.0	
Team: three/four people		
Design: in-house		
History: launched May 1995; redesigned December 1996; redesigned for new platform February 1998; e-commerce added May 1998; redesigned for new platform and spin-off sites added June 2000		
Monthly page views: 1.3 million for Cambridge International Dictionaries site; 850,000+ for catalogue site (http://uk.cambridge.org) Monthly sessions: 215,000 (catalogue site)		
Site size: 70,000+ pages		
Usability: not explicitly optimised, but generally suitable for Netscape 3.0		

The Cambridge University Press Web Sites

The Press has several web sites worldwide, covering a regional area (e.g. North America), a publishing strand (e.g. Cambridge Journals Online) or a business activity (e.g. printing services). The primary objective behind our Web presence is to support the publishing and printing activities of the Press through product promotion, information provision and sales generation. Although we do make a profit on-line, it is by increasing demand generally (e.g. by providing up-to-date stock levels, e-mail alerting, support materials and services to the trade), rather than by competing directly with existing channels, that we aim to make a difference.

In late 1999 we acquired the cambridge.org domain as a first step towards globalised web development, which will result in a common 'look and feel' across all our web sites. We felt that the situation then, of piecemeal, regional web development with a completely different user experience on each site, was detrimental to the brand as well as a potential waste of resources. The domain name was also desirable, in that it included the brand name as well as a global identifier. This case study covers the sites hosted and maintained in the UK, which were previously served from http://www.cup.cam.ac.uk and were the first to be re-branded.

During the specification phase we also decided to segment traffic channels into customer types by creating distinct sub-sites, namely:

- www.cambridge.org (portal site, launched in June 2000)
- uk.cambridge.org (the global catalogue site, e-commerce enabled, first launched in May 1995)
- booktrade.cambridge.org (services for the trade, e-commerce enabled, launched in June 2000)
- printing.cambridge.org (printing services, launched in June 2000)
- dictionary.cambridge.org (Cambridge Dictionaries Online, first launched in June 1999).

This segmentation of traffic enables us to service customers more effectively and aids in statistical reporting. In time other customer types – e.g. authors, librarians, learned societies – may also have sites developed for them as traffic continues to grow and new customer needs are identified and addressed.

All of the sites listed above were created in-house by a web unit comprising two small teams – one focusing on structure, content and design, and the other focusing on the interaction with core business systems and programming and support functions. The teams are co-ordinated by the Marketing and Information Services Manager.

We decided to change nearly everything – using live data (as opposed to weekly uploads), static pages, the complete catalogue (including out-of-print titles), improved e-commerce, richer catalogue information and more space for features and promotions. This created a series of challenges, which broadly fall into the areas of design, structure and technical implementation.

Design

This was the longest phase of development, for a variety of reasons. Before a mouse was clicked in anger we took a long look at what we wanted to do, by visiting competitor sites, popular e-commerce and information sites and finally the best-of-breed design sites. This was to establish what our core audience expected in specific areas (such as button naming, sizing and positioning), and, more importantly, where we needed to be different.

We decided to keep it as simple, and as 'standard' as possible, aiming at a target resolution of 640 × 480, left alignment and version 3 browsers and above, with little or no Flash, JavaScript or HTML 4+. Site statistics showed that we could have gone higher (more than 95 percent of all sessions were version 4 browsers or higher), but with more than 500 different agent tags visiting monthly we felt it was better to get the basics right. If time and resources permit we will revisit certain areas later – or purchase a content management solution to help target specific platforms, e.g. WAP (wireless application protocol), text only.

Next we identified page 'types', drew them up on paper and marked areas out in pseudo-XML (extensible markup language). In most cases we created 'idealised types' – making allowances for content or design elements that we knew would not be there for the launch, such as product banners. We also drew out links between pages, creating matrices and Venn diagrams to help us picture groups of pages 'working together'.

At this stage we decided on some key concepts: logo on every page, colour themes for the different product groups, white background, black text (with Verdana specified as the preferred font), a base colour for use on the home page and site-specific logos and buttons. As most of the advertising for the site would be done by subject-specific or territory-specific marketing colleagues we decided to give them ownership of certain aspects of the design (namely background images on subject pages and choice of colour theme); this helped to create goodwill internally and increased the range of images for which we have electronic permissions.

The design, therefore, is an application of rules and styles that make it relatively straightforward to create new pages, construct 'types' out of styles and also present a strong and consistent brand message. It is also self-referential, in that the design manual is itself a series of web pages composed according to these rules, and forms the basis of all web development, both internal and external.

The consistent application of these styles has increased the speed of content production and also allows us to concentrate our design resources more on graphic creation and less on page layout. Thus the web designers concentrate on creating feature modules (micro-sites) for re-use on all Press web sites, and the marketing department can create basic pages with a minimum of training and supervision.

Revisions happen constantly, and we already have a portfolio of tweaks to implement on the next revamp. Ultimately this approach saves both time and effort and will ease the inevitable transition to a full XML mark-up/content management system over time.

Structure

The process of creating the broad structure for the catalogue site was fairly straightforward and would probably apply to any number of products, not just books. There is an area for people with a general interest in the brand or a subject ('browse'); a facility for people to get to information they already know they want ('search'); and areas of 'corporate' information and news for 'prospects' (the don't knows and the mildly curious) – authors, students, media (the ubiquitous 'about us').

The subject classification caused great internal consternation – rather than be tied to our existing (budgetary) coding, or use complex standards such as BIC (Book Industry Communication, http://www.bic.org.uk) that don't necessarily work internationally or across all subjects, we decided to create an entirely new subject structure. Using a parent–child methodology we arrived at a list of top-level subjects that was as customer-friendly as possible. Each subject site has its own entry point to the catalogue site, making it more attractive for the marketing department to include in publicity and encouraging the association of brand and subject, e.g. the 'Cambridge Economics' page, not 'an economics page on the Cambridge University Press site'.

Each subject site can have the following areas: catalogue, e-mail list, features page and associated modules, resources page, bestsellers list, reading room, publicity downloads and, most importantly, any number of 'children' (which can be thought of as individual publishing lists), which we term sections.

Examples of subject sections include:

- Psychology > Cognitive Psychology
- ELT > Products > Courses for Younger Learners > Cambridge English for Schools
- Bibles > Gift Editions

We could, in theory, have a section for 'green hardbacks, by Polish authors, that went out of print in 1976', but fortunately that was never proposed.

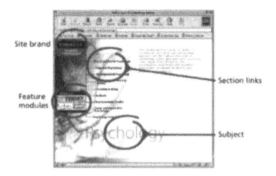

A subject site home page.

Each section can have none or all of the following items: catalogue list, highlights list, textbooks list, news, events, awards list.

A section can belong to a number of sites, and an individual title can appear in many sections and on more than one site.

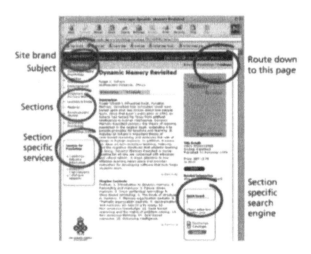

A catalogue page demonstrating section styling.

This creates a standard yet flexible offering across the whole list, encourages cross-promotion of titles in different sections and makes it easy to promote titles systematically; for example, the scheduling of highlights and news can be input well ahead of schedule and called out automatically by a program. In theory this should make it more attractive to re-visit the site, as information will be constantly changing and will be more relevant to the customer because they will have selected their interests themselves.

Technical Implementation

The changes outlined above, coupled with a need for live data (for stock levels and e-commerce) and static pages, created an enormous strain on our technical resources, and have caused numerous problems since the site went live. We were over-ambitious, to put it mildly.

The biggest single change for the site was the move to a live database – previously we had 'published' to a relatively small and straightforward SQL server on a weekly basis. With a new and untested system, in hindsight we should have waited for the Oracle solution to bed down properly. The pressure to re-launch our site (it was replacing a site launched in February 1998) was such that we felt compelled to go live in that it was 'good enough'. Since the launch there have been numerous problems, not least the daily downtime while the Oracle database is rebuilt from all the host sources – and because most of the site depends on the core data being correct this has meant that the site has not worked as intended.

Principally this is because we wanted to 'publish' title pages as and when changes to the data occurred, e.g. as publications came back in stock, or new reviews were added. Published (static) pages are preferable both for performance and statistics collation. They are also easier to link to, which was important because we knew that our authors' sites generated a large proportion of the traffic to our site.

The static page generation is achieved by software (XBuilder) calling ASP scripts that pick up design elements (based on site structure tables in the core database) and product data. It is effectively impossible to rebuild the site daily, so a hugely inefficient weekly build of the entire catalogue (70,000 pages!) has to be done to keep the static site moderately up to date.

We had been using Muscat to index these static pages, and tags to create a 'just in time' database of core bibliographic data and details of where and how a page should display in a search list. It had been thought that Muscat's natural language searching would always present the best material on any title to the searcher (i.e. when we had a feature or a sample it would present that entry before the catalogue entry). Muscat is also an excellent concept-based search tool.

However, we have since discovered that the vast majority of searching on our site is highly specific, and thus is far more suited to Boolean searching. Muscat can do this, but it wastes a lot of its potential. Coupled with the need to re-index thousands of pages daily, the Muscat search engine is currently not particularly efficient and is proving to be highly unpopular. This will hopefully change as the core systems improve to enable us to use Muscat to its full potential.

Another huge issue was the complexity of the structure. Eventually we decided to limit the catalogues to one per subject (whereas initially we had had one per section) and also to restrict to one the number of levels of children. There are still sections at lower levels but these cause problems for the page-generation scripts, which were designed for a one-to-one relationship.

On a happier note, we are expecting a new Oracle system to go live in November 2000; this system will be the source of data and not just the host, and won't require a daily rebuild. This will enable us to build pages only when data changes, and not just in case it's changed. The new Oracle system will offer us more reliability, contain richer data and open up the possibility of offering new functionality, such as order tracking and order history.

Overall this is a very different site from anything we've had before, and we feel it is reasonably distinctive among publisher sites. Because we first modelled the site on paper, and created relationships between content and styles that were subsequently regrouped as pages, it meant, in effect, that the build process was akin to playing with Lego. The transition to a theory- and rules-based construction means that we have the building blocks to create any number of sites and pages in an organic, controlled fashion at relatively low cost and with little fuss.

Which means, unfortunately, that our work has only just begun.

The Faculty and Institute of Actuaries

(http://www.actuaries.org.uk)

The UK actuarial profession has two professional bodies: the Faculty of Actuaries in Scotland, and the Institute of Actuaries covering the rest of the UK. The profession has 5,700 student members and 6,700 qualified members, and is supported by the unified staff of both organisations. Approximately one-third of all members are based outside the UK. In the past actuaries worked mainly in life insurance and pensions, but today they also work in business and finance where they apply their skills in evaluating and managing financial risk.

The profession's web site was launched in 1996, with the initial aim of reaching potential new recruits. Since then it has expanded into a comprehensive information resource aimed at all members and at the public, with over 2,000 pages attracting around 45,000 requests for pages per week.

By Sally Grover (Web Master) and Emma Pegg (Web Site Administrator)

Frames: yes	JavaScript: yes	Java: no
Flash: no	Audio/video: not yet	Animation: no
HTML editor: HomeSite 4.0		
Database: DB/Text WebPublisher (library database), mSQL (members database)		
FTP: CuteFTP	Graphics: Paint Shop Pro 6	
Server software: UNIX, Apache Virtual Server		
Team: one-third-time web master, two-thirds-time administrator, plus help from IT department (e.g. with analysis of site statistics and technical issues)		
Design: Oxford CommUnity Internet plc (OCI)		
History: launched April 1996; latest redesign October 1999		
Monthly page views: 180,000		
Site size: 2,000 pages		
Usability: optimised for Netscape 4, Internet Explorer 4, Adobe Acrobat 4		

The Institute of Actuaries' web site is a key component of the profession's e-business strategy, which is to provide services – both information and transactions – to its members, and to the public, that are cost-effective and accessible, easy to use and integrated, accurate and secure. While raising the profile of a relatively small profession and encouraging suitable new recruits remain important objectives, a recent goal has been for the site to provide an enhanced level of service to members.

The site has been hosted by OCI, who undertook the last two redesigns, since 1998. The site is developed through the Internet strategy committee, a group of eight actuaries and four staff. As web master, I [Sally Grover] am secretary to this committee and responsible for implementing its recommendations. In 1996 I took the post after one day's training in HTML, and with a laptop plugged into a phone line. Within four years something that started out as a pioneering initiative has become a widely accepted communications medium. The site now has an administrator, who carries out the maintenance, updating and reporting, and a fast connection via our 128 kb ISDN dial-up connection (soon to become a 2 Mb leased line).

Managing Content and Encouraging Use

Develop procedures for updating the site and adding new material. Encourage a sense of ownership among those who contribute information.

The profession transacts its business through a series of boards. Each board comprises members, who are actuaries, and a secretary, who is a senior member of staff. The boards focus on the areas in which actuaries work, for example life insurance, pensions, finance and investment and social policy. A separate board is responsible for education and the continuing professional development of members. The boards are the ultimate owners of most of the material on the site. The rest of the material, for example the staff contact list, the 'what's new' page and the list of the 30 most frequently visited pages, is the direct responsibility of the web site team (the web master and site administrator).

Once the site was launched, in 1996, an increasing volume of material began to arrive for publication on the site. The following list indicates the range of material:

- Press releases
- Responses to consultation documents
- Position statements (statements of the profession's position on specific issues)
- Lists of members and terms of reference for all boards and committees
- Guidance notes

- Past exam papers and reports
- News pages
- Newsletters
- Contents pages and abstracts of papers from the *British Actuarial Journal*
- Conference papers
- Working party reports
- Conference announcements
- Job adverts.

Initial estimates of the complexity of preparing web pages and maintaining an ever-expanding site were optimistic: 'You just take a Word document, press "save as HTML" and hey presto, don't you?' Since no additional resource had been allocated for the maintenance of the site, updates sometimes fell into arrears. The initial proposal was that each department would assume responsibility for maintaining its own section of the site: designated individuals would be given training in HTML and direct access to upload their own pages. A comprehensive training programme was organised and representatives from all departments, from the Chief Executive downwards, were trained. The results were dramatic: it was rapidly realised that web page preparation could not simply be added to the already heavy workloads. Even the Chief Executive had second thoughts after a close encounter with the tag!

A new proposal involved the appointment of an experienced secretary as web administrator, with responsibility for monitoring the site and ensuring that new information was posted and general areas were kept up-to-date. This person had previously worked in our public relations department and already had a comprehensive understanding of the organisation's work. However, the staff who knew what information had to go onto their part of the site still had to remain responsible for generating that material and for telling the administrator when to remove items. In addition a web site management group, which comprises representatives from all departments that contribute information to the site, meets every 2–3 months to contribute ideas for the operation and development of the site. This group is evolving as a forum for creative thinking about the site and is developing a strong sense of ownership.

The Current Site Management Model

Strategy

Committee: **Internet strategy committee**

Chair:	An actuary
Members:	Eight actuaries representing the boards; editor of *The Actuary*; four members of staff
Committee secretary:	Web master
Objectives:	• To ensure that Internet technology, including the web site, is fully exploited to further the aims of the profession and meet the profession's needs
	• To monitor the use, content and development of the site
	• To monitor the budget.

Staff: **Web master**

Previous experience:	Librarian
Responsibilities:	• To implement the strategy agreed by the Internet strategy committee
	• To manage and develop the site to meet the needs and expectations of the profession.

Operation

Committee: **Web site management group**

Chair:	Web master
Members:	Ten members of staff representing the departments that contribute information to the site
Committee secretary:	Site administrator
Objectives:	• To promote the good operation of the web site and staff intranet, including procedures, layouts, briefing, training and resources
	• To disseminate information about the web site and intranet to staff and to co-ordinate staff input
	• To provide a forum for ideas to improve and develop both the intranet and the web site.

Staff: **Site administrator**

Previous experience: Secretary and PA in the PR department

Responsibilities:
- To update the information on the site
- To prompt owners of pages for new material
- To maintain the site map, etc.
- To prepare briefing bulletins on new information added to the site.

Site Publicity

The web site is a key part of the organisation's strategy for achieving better communication with its members. This strategy has two prongs:

- providing significant content
- encouraging a culture of electronic communication.

As explained above, the initiative to provide new information lies with the board secretaries. However, the site administrator plays a proactive role in monitoring the site, and prompts the secretaries when information looks outdated and when she is aware that new information has been issued.

A programme of site publicity aims to bring the site and its resources to the attention of both members and staff. Features on the site to help members identify new and popular material include a 'what's new' page, with direct links to new information, and a 'top 30 most popular pages' list. A fortnightly e-mail bulletin of new additions is circulated to all staff and a regular column entitled 'Have you visited the web site recently?' is published in *The Actuary* magazine.

The need to provide professional information to members only, and to allow certain subsets of members access to committee agendas and papers and advance conference papers, is being addressed in the third redesign of the site. The new site will be dynamically generated so that once visitors have registered they will automatically be admitted to the areas they are authorised to visit.

Some Practical Challenges

Promoting the Profession
Decide whether your site will accept sponsorship or advertising and draw up guidelines.

An opportunity to enhance the site arose in 1998 on the occasion of the 150th anniversary of the Institute's foundation. An exhibition on the actuarial profession, past, present and future, was presented at the Institute's hall at Staple Inn, High Holborn, and at other venues around the country. The exhibition acted as a focus for corporate hospitality and for visits by sixth-formers, university students, mathematics teachers and members of the public. The organising committee felt that the exhibition would benefit from the inclusion of some interactive computer models to enable younger visitors to experience at first-hand the decision processes that an actuary goes through in the course of his or her daily work.

Finance was a concern until a generous and unexpected approach was received from Swiss Re, who offered to sponsor part of the site in return for a direct link to their home page. The agreement with Swiss Re to sponsor the development of three interactive models illustrating different aspects of actuarial work was concluded on 6 April 1998. The models ran on a UNIX web server at the exhibition venues and after the exhibition closed they were made available on the web site; under the terms of the agreement there was to be a link to Swiss Re's home page for at least one year. The exhibition, complete with models, opened in Birmingham on 7 June 1998. The models were developed by a group of actuaries and designed and programmed in JavaScript by Chris King of OCI. They are still on the site (at http://www.actuaries.org.uk/interactives/index.html), and illustrate aspects of demographic change, the effects of different investment strategies on a pension fund and the management of a life insurance company. They contrast with the pages of text on the site and give the visitor a practical insight into the work of

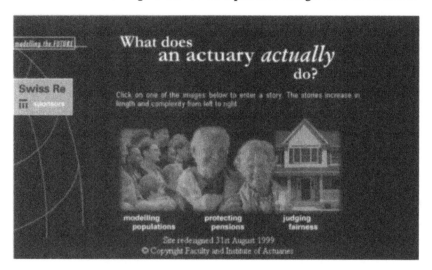

Screen shot from interactive section of web site.

an actuary. The profession believes that overt sponsorship of the site is not compatible with the independent image that a profession should have, but it has since set up a sponsorship committee to give due consideration to any future sponsorship opportunities.

Services to Students
If you are anticipating huge demands on your site, ensure that you have adequate bandwidth.

As an organisation with 5,700 students (one-third of whom are outside the UK), which sets and marks its own exams, the web site plays a crucial role when the exam results are released. Soon after the site was launched in 1996 students asked for results to be published on the site. However, our service provider at that time did not have sufficient bandwidth to deal with thousands of simultaneous accesses, and many students were frustrated and angry at being unable to access the pages. This experience prompted us to transfer the site to our current service provider, OCI, who have a comfortable 40 mb of bandwidth. In addition, OCI arrange for the complete site to be mirrored on a server in the US, which overseas students are advised to bookmark. The exam results are also posted on the sites of the Actuarial Society of South Africa and the Society of Actuaries in Ireland. The results pages are uploaded to a secure area of the server the day before they are due to be released and copied over to the public area automatically at midnight. The students, despite some initial misgivings about others possibly knowing their results before they do, are pleased that they don't have to rely on the postal services or on telephoning the exams department. The system, as it currently operates, has never failed, and in theory the web master could have an early night ...

Databases
Keep an open mind when seeking solutions.

The profession maintains a library database catalogue using DB/Text WebPublisher, a textbase management package developed by InMagic, Inc., and distributed in the UK by Soutron Ltd. The database comprises around 21,500 records of books, conference proceedings, reports and journal articles. Members, especially those based overseas, asked for the database to be made available on the site. As the site already included a bookshop it seemed at good opportunity to link the two together, thereby providing a better service to members. Even if a library book is out on loan, a copy might be available for purchase; and if a book is out of stock in the bookshop, it might be available on loan from the library.

Initially we considered a bespoke solution from our service provider. However, it became apparent that the size and complexity of the bibliographic records were such that a bespoke solution would be costly. The decision was therefore taken to publish the catalogue using DB/Text

WebPublisher. The drawback to this solution was that our existing service provider could not host the database because it only runs under Windows NT, and our provider used UNIX servers. However, Soutron Ltd offer a web-hosting service and we decided that they would host the database, enabling us to benefit from their expertise with Windows NT. DB/Text WebPublisher will also be used to set up a research database, with members of working parties entering data directly onto the site.

Final Thoughts ...

Overall, it has been a period of fun, frustration and challenge. One ongoing challenge remains the need to encourage some staff and actuaries to look at the site as a valuable communication medium and not just as another addition to an already heavy workload. The site has to support the whole profession and we need to make it easy for busy actuaries to get straight to what they need while at the same time tempting other visitors to dip in and learn about a fascinating and little-understood profession.

Useful Resources

Web Sites
Webmonkey (http://hotwired.lycos.com/webmonkey/)
The web developer's resource; very clear, step-by-step tutorials

Books
Musciano, C. and Kennedy, B. *HTML & XHTML: The Definitive Guide,* 4th edition, Sebastopol, California, O'Reilly & Associates, 2000

Chapter 3

Page Design and Graphics

After the planning and site design stages, the next step is to decide on a clear, consistent set of page layouts which guide the visitor through the content of the site. Appropriate graphics and added features should enhance the visitor experience by adding to the understanding of the content without delaying access to that content.

Page Styles, Graphics and Formats

To present information in a manner that is comprehensible, you need to use a variety of presentation techniques. A long scrolling page of text with no formatting at all is extremely hard – and boring – to read and understand. By building a visual hierarchy on the page, using text formatting, headings and graphics, you will help the reader assess and understand the importance of the different elements on the page.

Effective page layout depends on differentiating the various elements on the page, which may include:

- Page and section headings
- Navigation links
- Main content
- Related content links (other articles, next page, etc.)
- Advertising images or links
- Subsidiary content (copyright, disclaimers, creation date, etc.).

Page and Section Headings

The heading on a page should provide instant confirmation to the visitor that they have come to the page they expected when they followed the previous link. Size, position and typography should separate the heading from the main body content as well as distinguishing it from other top-level information, such as the name of the site, which might also appear on every page.

Remember that visitors might arrive at this page 'cold', directly from a search engine result or from an external link, with no previous visual memory of your design or layout. Ensure that the heading relates to the text following, and provide clues to the structure of the page as a whole – can a reader just look at the heading and understand the key points on the page? Best typographic practice also indicates that a heading should not be all upper case as this is harder to read than normal sentence case (capital first letter, then lower case).

Navigation Links

As well as providing a means of accessing the rest of the site, the links should also help distinguish between the major site links and those in the same directory as the current page. Some sites do this by putting the top-level links across the top and bottom of the page, with the current directory links down the left-hand margin. On other sites all links are listed in the left-hand margin, but sub-menus are in a different size font from the directory links. Yet another option is to use folder tabs to create a very separate hierarchy of links.

Main Content

This is of course the most important element of the page, and should be designed for maximum usability – large blocks of plain text do not work as well as fully formatted content that includes headings, bullets, indentations and illustrations. Long sections might be better broken in to several pages.

Navigation Rules
'Navigation normally has three tiers:

- global (site-wide) on all pages
- sectional with different buttons for each section and indicating the section that the user is in
- local for a page which may simply have a "return to top" button or a contents list with anchors in the text.

Try to keep the number of buttons or options for the top two tiers to less than seven, as more may be confusing.'

Elaine Robinson
Freelance Web Developer

Related Content Links

These are links that appear either within the text or in a sidebar, and guide the reader to related articles on the same topic (essentially a selection from the archive). They will normally be plain text links, as they will be specific to that page's content, rather than being repeated throughout the directory.

Advertising Images or Links

If the site has advertising images, or affiliate links, these should be designed so that they are not confused with the core content. Normally this is not a problem, as they will carry the logo and colours of the advertiser, but affiliate links to rele-

Navigation Panels with ASP and INC
'Sites are moving away from the use of frames to separate navigation from content because of difficulties with indexing by search engines and targeting external links to dynamically generated ASP pages. You can still maintain the code for your navigation panel in a separate, easily updatable file by saving it as an INC or ASP file and using the server include instruction to insert it in every ASP page, e.g. <!–# INCLUDE FILE="NAV.ASP" –>'

Elaine Robinson
Freelance Web Developer

vant titles on Amazon or other booksellers, for example, should not be too similar to the related content links described above.

Subsidiary Content

The previous chapter referred to those elements that you might wish to include on a page – they will normally be in smaller font and, although important from a corporate or legal point of view, they are less important to the understanding of that page's content.

Tone and Style

The literary style and conversational tone you use in the text should match the reader's expectations – depending on the topic of the site and the page this might be chatty or authoritative, cheerful or serious. Use of slang, jargon and clichés must be carefully judged so as not to irritate, offend or confuse. A fast medium such as the Web needs shorter sentences. Your style should be clear, simple and direct, perhaps with less waffle than might be allowed in print.

Consistency

Use the same capitalisations and the same technical terms throughout to avoid confusion. Similarly, use consistent page and paragraph layouts and spacing across the site, to give the impression that a single editorial team is responsible for the content, rather than a number of individuals.

Font Selection

Although there are some fonts designed specifically for the computer screen, such as Georgia and Verdana (quite similar to Times New Roman and Arial respectively, but generally better spaced and clearer), most users do not change their default settings. However, the browser can be set to ignore styles defined within the HTML document. Also your visitor's computer will only display fonts available in the system font directory. What this all adds up to is a lack of certainty as to how visitors will see your pages. Most will see them as you have designed them to be seen, but there will always be a proportion that do not.

The <font> command lets you specify a series of fonts, and the browser will look for each in turn before defaulting to the base font if none of the specified fonts are found. However, you should always ask yourself if it is useful to require the visitor to see your pages in an unfamiliar font, or in one that their system may simply not have. You should also check the different display characteristics of PCs and Macs, which can show the same font at very different sizes. For absolute control over typeface and size you may need to create a graphic rather than depend on the limited control provided within HTML. Extra graphics will have implications for page loading speeds, however, and so should only be chosen after careful consideration.

Style Sheets

To establish and maintain a consistent style across your site, it can be useful to create a set of printed style sheets for each page type. Most web sites will have three or four basic page types for navigation, content and product pages, as well as the home page. Variations in the pages' appearance can be minimised by providing everyone who might edit or create pages with a style sheet that establishes column widths, font types and sizes, background and accent colours as well as editorial styles – abbreviations, naming conventions and spelling standards (British or American English, for example).

> **Quick Site Creation**
> 'Site creation is easy using templates and style sheets. You can quickly implement a design by creating a template in a package like Dreamweaver. Each page is then created from a template that contains locked, un-editable areas for items such as navigation bars and logos that appear on every page, and editable regions for the text. Couple this with a style sheet where basic HTML tags, e.g. <h1>, <h2>, are redefined with new styles, and then just apply the correct tags to the text.'
>
> **Elaine Robinson**
> **Freelance Web Developer**

This style sheet can be combined with a library of approved graphics, each with a specified height and width, to ensure that no maverick logos are used. By building the graphics and style sheet into an on-line template for each page type you not only maximise consistency, but you also reduce the effort involved in adding new content.

Cascading style sheets (CSS) let you implement the same idea on a web page: by setting styles that define how each tag will look, and by linking to the CSS from each page, you can ensure a consistent look and feel to your site. And making changes to a style is simple, as you only need to change the parent style sheet file for the rest of the site to pick up the new look.

> 'If you use cascading style sheets you can make one change to the style sheet which updates the entire site. A great time saver.'
>
> **Matt Martel**
> **ContentGenerators**

Page Layout

HTML has developed enormously since its original conception as a means of describing document structure. Like it or not, it is now seen and used as much more a visual display language – and not a very flexible one at that. Nevertheless, you can take advantage of some of the normal design principles of desktop publishing and use

> **Browser Offset**
> 'If you're having trouble aligning buttons and text with a background image, or if you just want your page to start in the top left corner of the browser window, then here are the commands to remove the varying page offsets that different browsers apply. In the <body> tag include topmargin="0", leftmargin="0" for Internet Explorer, and marginwidth="0", marginheight="0" for Netscape.'
>
> **Elaine Robinson**
> **Freelance Web Developer**

clear white space, wide margins and multiple columns to create a pleasing layout.

The left-hand index column is a standard design. If you ever see a page with the index links on the right-hand side of the page, you will realise abruptly how much you expect to see them on the left. Because we read from left to right it is natural for the eye to fall on the left-hand side of the screen; and because HTML allows the right-hand side of the screen to wrap if column and table widths are not specified, the left-hand side can be the only margin guaranteed to remain consistent.

Page Width

One golden rule of web page design is to avoid horizontal scrolling. In some circumstances this can be particularly difficult, for example if you need to display a large graphic or table of data, but in the vast majority of cases horizontal scrolling is caused by thoughtless design. If you use a monitor set at a high resolution (1024×768, 1152×864, or even higher), then a page that fits nicely on to your monitor will almost inevitably stretch beyond the limits of the monitors used by the majority of your audience.

TheCounter.com (http://www.thecounter.com) provides free hit counters to thousands of web sites, and from the statistical returns from all its users it has produced a table of monitor preferences. This gives a strong indication of the likely settings you should test your pages at to guarantee clear display without scrolling.

'Make allowances for various screen display settings when creating templates or pages, e.g. 640×480, 800×600 or 1024768. There is nothing more frustrating than viewing a website which goes off the screen (i.e. you have to scroll across to see the rest of the page) or has vast amounts of white space.'

Doreen Louvre
REFUND Project, University of Newcastle upon Tyne

'Create sites with a 15-inch screen in mind or face the peril of losing half the audience. Simple but essential.'

Gary Catchpole
Creative Director, Eye Design

Monitor resolution statistics from theCounter.com for September 2000 (based on 458.9 million page views)	
Resolution	Percentage of users
800×600	55
1024×768	28
640×480	8
1280×1024	2
1152×864	2
Unknown	1
1600×1200	>1

Source: theCounter.com (http://www.thecounter.com)

This shows that if you design at 800 × 600, you risk giving users with monitors set at 640 × 80 (8 percent of overall users) a less than perfect experience. Conversely, if your monitor is set at higher than 800 × 600 then you may leave over 60 per cent of your visitors with a bad impression! You will need to make a judgement on whether 92 per cent of visitors is an adequate target for your design, or if you need to try to design for that extra

> **Scaling Pages**
> 'Designing for a particular monitor size and screen resolution using exact pixel widths often means poor use of the screen with lots of white space at higher resolutions. You can use a table with proportional cell widths stated in percentages, e.g. <td width = "60%">, so that your page scales to the screen size. You can mix exact pixel widths, e.g. in a column of buttons, with scaling widths for the other columns.'
>
> **Elaine Robinson**
> **Freelance Web Developer**

8 per cent. Commercial organisations might take the view that users with older monitors set to 640 × 480 are not their core target audience. Educational, charity or government sites might set themselves higher targets. This is not about excluding visitors – it is just a risk that a small percentage might see your site in a marginally more inconvenient way.

What this means in terms of page layout is that you will need to specify the width of your tables and columns in such a way as to ensure that they fit in the screen for the vast majority of your users – and where practical, of course, for all users. If you specify <table width="100%"> then the browser will keep the width of the table to the size of the open window – but this will be over-ridden if the columns contain items that cannot wrap, such as graphics. When the combined width of the widest graphic in each column is larger than 800 pixels, then setting a table width will not prevent horizontal scrolling on a monitor set at a resolution of 800 × 600 pixels.

If you set cell widths using the width attribute of the <td> command, perhaps to control the width of an index column so it is only as wide as the navigation links, leave the width of the main cell undefined, to allow for wrapping. This will provide all users with a

> 'For most browser-friendly web sites, put your content in one or more tables, and centre those tables. Nothing looks as poorly designed as a left-justified 600-pixel-wide site in a 1024-pixel-wide browser window.'
>
> **George Edw. Seymour**
> **Systems Information Resources**

full screen of content, whereas <table width="800"> will give users with higher resolution settings clear space beside the table – set the table to be in the centre of the screen if you don't want a large margin to the right of the screen. Ensuring that at least one column contains only wrappable content – e.g. text – or has no graphics wide enough to cause a problem should guarantee an acceptable page display.

If your pages are designed to be printed, or if you think that your users will be likely to print them out, then you may need to limit the table width even further, perhaps to as little as 500–530 pixels, to ensure that the full content will fit on to an A4 page. By providing printable versions of the pages, essentially the text without the navigation or advertising graphics, you can get around the design limitations implied by designing the same page for both screen and print.

Page Length

This is less of an issue, as vertical scrolling is often unavoidable. However, it is generally accepted practice to put the important navigational information 'above the fold' – in other words, in the first screen of the page. Home pages, navigation pages and pages with interactive tools and forms should generally be designed to fit in a single screen – the user needs to see at a glance what his or her options are.

> 'People hate to wait.
> People hate to scroll.
> People hate to read.
> People would rather scroll than wait.
> People would rather wait than read.
> People are not necessarily rational or consistent, but sometimes they are.'
>
> **David Supple**
> **External Relations and**
> **Development Office,**
> **Birmingham University**

Long documents should be broken down in to several linked pages, as this is easier for the user to read and pages load quicker. But provide a single printable version without the navigation links or other non-document content for those who prefer their documents to be on paper.

Frames

Another method of achieving a column effect on your page is by using frames, where the different files are called up and assembled within a frameset layout. Frames have their critics and their adherents, with good reasons on both sides.

Advantages	Disadvantages
• Site maintenance	• Printing and saving
• Design consistency	• Bookmarks/favourites
• Narrative flow	• Screen space
• Interactivity	• Design errors.

Advantages

Site Maintenance
By separating out the navigation and content, you only need to update the index file when adding new sections to a site. On non-framed sites, each page would need to be updated.

Design Consistency

By fixing the navigation file, and perhaps by having another frame as a title or masthead, you can ensure a rigid consistency across the site. The masthead can of course be set to adjust for each section of the site.

Narrative Flow

When displaying long documents, a series of images, poems or instructions, you can use a frame to hold the table of content, so that users can click through the items one at a time without reloading the entire page.

Interactivity

Frames can be used to enhance the interactive nature of a site: a calculating tool can show the result in a frame, allowing repeat calculations without the need to go back to the entry page. Movies can be shown in a separate frame, again giving the viewer the option of working through a list.

Disadvantages

Printing and Saving

The very nature of frames causes problems in saving and printing – each frame is a separate file, which typically needs to be saved or printed separately. However, the current versions of the browsers can cope with this, so it is less of an issue than it used to be.

Bookmarks/Favourites

Because the parent URL is normally displayed throughout a visitor session, adding a particular page within a site to the bookmark or favourites file is impossible without opening that page up in a new window – but that will then lose the navigational links.

Screen Space

Where frames are wider or longer than the setting allowed for in the frameset definition, scrollbars will take up substantial screen space. This will happen even more for users with low-resolution monitors, giving them an even worse visitor experience.

Design Errors

Scrolling and resizing can be removed by using the scrolling="no" and resize="0" options. This may clean up the screen appearance, but if the content is larger than the space provided there will be no way for the user to scroll or resize so as to see that content.

Graphics Considerations

For the typical content-driven web site, graphics have one purpose and one purpose only – to enhance the delivery of information. This might be by illustrating the text, or by providing navigation links. The rule of thumb is that if a graphic can be removed from a page without impairing its meaning or functionality, then it should be taken out. Every graphic added to a page slows down the loading of that page just a little. Ill-chosen or badly designed graphics can slow down a page so much that the user loses patience and goes elsewhere before the page is completely visible.

Safe Colours

There may be over 16 million colours available to the vast majority of Web users, but there are still some users whose monitors show only 256 colours. The GIF format supports only 256 colours.

> 'Colour-blind people can only read your text if the colours have sufficient contrast. Convert the background hex codes into decimals and add up the red, green and blue components. Do the same for the text colour. The results must differ by at least 255. For example: bgcolor="#339900" >>> 51+153+0 = 204; text="#0066cc" >>> 0+102+204=306; 306–204=102 >>> not enough contrast.'
> **Beccy Manley**
> **KidStuff**

Netscape and Internet Explorer, on a PC or Mac, use a colour management system that effectively supports just 216 colours, with the other 40 being used by the operating system for icons and buttons. The result is that there are only 216 colours guaranteed to display as you expect. The implication of this is that you need, as far as possible, to ensure that your graphics are created using the 'safe' colour palette, in order to avoid dithering or speckling of areas of colour.

Number of monitor colours	Percentage of users
65,000 (16 bit)	54
(32 bit)	25
16 million (24 bit)	12
256 (8 bit)	7
16 (4 bit)	0.05

Source: theCounter.com (http://www.thecounter.com)

The suggested strategy is to ensure that all your navigation link images, saved as GIFs, are created using the safe colour palette, while photographic images in JPG format have a higher number of colours which will display perfectly in most monitors, but in those with lower colour settings will be dithered or reduced, perhaps limiting the quality of the image.

The Visibone Color Laboratory (http://www.visibone.com/colorlab/) provides a number of tools to help designers pick safe colours: the one illustrated below is a colour wheel. It allows you to select contrasting and complementary colours and see how they appear on other colours, to ensure that the text and links will be visible against the chosen colour background.

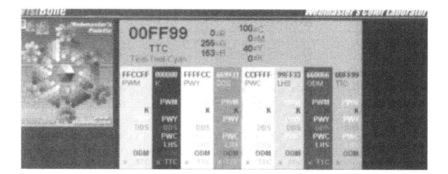

Pixellation

To avoid your GIF images looking pixellated (having jagged edges), keep the lines and edges horizontal, vertical or at 45-degree angles.

Animations

As few animations really add much to the understanding of a page, it is best to avoid them where possible. They are usually larger files, and can be very distracting to the reader. If you are using an animation to demonstrate a process, or as a flow chart, then it may be more appropriate to place it in a separate page. If it is left within a content page set it to loop just once, or perhaps twice, rather than continuously. The idea, as always, is to enhance rather than to confuse or distract the user.

Optimising Graphics
'PhotoShop 5.5 has a save for Web" option which simplifies the process of optimising graphics and results in very small files sizes. A 4-up view lets you choose the number of colours, type of palette (selective, adaptive, etc), dither, etc., and compare the results before saving. You can easily preview in different browsers and even choose browser dither" to simulate the appearance on a monitor with 256 colours. ImageReady and Fireworks have similar optimisation options.'

Elaine Robinson
Freelance Web Designer

Converting Graphics

When scanning or saving graphic files, bear in mind that Mac monitors display only 72 dots per inch (dpi), whilst PC monitors show 96 dpi. Creating graphics at higher dpi settings is wasteful, as the monitor cannot display them at their full resolution and the file size will be much higher. One major exception would be if they are designed for printing, as 300 dpi would more closely match the printer output quality.

Simple Graphics Optimisation Checklist

- Save graphics as GIFs and photographs as JPGs to get the best compression of the file size
- Use the same bullet image for a bulleted list – the browser only has to download a single image and repeat it, rather than download several different ones

- Reduce the number of colours used in link graphics as far as possible to ensure each is the smallest possible file size

- Check your images in a service such as GifWizard or NetMechanic to see if they can be compressed further without affecting their appearance

- Specify height and width attributes for every image to speed up the page display by the browser.

> 'Macromedia Fireworks wins every time – it produces top-quality images which compress beautifully. Many graphics packages generate bitmap files, but Fireworks generates vector-based files which are much smaller, even before compression.'
>
> **Judith Bonser**
> **Onion Productions**

Invisible Pixel Tricks

In a graphics package such as PhotoShop or Paint Shop Pro, create an image one pixel high by one pixel wide. Set the colour to be transparent, thus creating an invisible image. By setting height and width attributes this invisible pixel can be used in a number of ways:

> 'A good way of creating a site design is to use a graphics package (e.g. Photoshop, Fireworks) to prepare a graphic of a page or pages with all the backgrounds, buttons, logos, etc. you need. Once the design has been finalised you can easily "slice and dice" it into separate buttons, etc., using ImageReady or Fireworks, or by dragging guides from the rulers in Photoshop and selecting the area with "snap to guides" on.'
>
> **Elaine Robinson**
> **Freelance Web Designer**

- `<img src="pixel.gif" height="1" width="10">` to create a paragraph indent

- `<img src="pixel.gif" height="1" width="1" border="0">` to provide invisible links to the home page from doorway pages (see Chapter 6)

- `<img src="pixel.gif" height="1" width="1" hspace="10">` to create space within a line of text

- `<img src="pixel.gif" height="10" width="1">` to create controlled vertical space between a heading and text without using the `<h1>` command (which will put a line of space above and below the heading)

- `<img src="pixel.gif" height="10" width="10" border="2">` to create a checkbox in a printable form

- `<img src="pixel.gif" height="1" width="1" alt="keyword">` as a slightly underhand method of including a few more keywords in a document (see Chapter 6)

- In all cases except the last, use alt=" " to 'disappear' the image from page readers (see Chapter 4).

When deciding on the level of technology to use in developing and delivering your web site, consider the following:

- **Does it help deliver the content?**

Converting all text to graphics may add little in terms of meaning, but slow down the delivery and reduce accessibility. Do you need database output, or a Shockwave animation? Can you do without?

> 'Less is more: keep it simple. Cute little flashy busy things get very tiresome after a while. You wouldn't do it at home, be very careful of doing it on a Web site.
> If the design is clear, you need fewer gimmicks to grab people's attention.'
>
> **Liz Citron**
> **MD, Arehaus**

- **Can the audience cope?**

Will they have the appropriate plug-in, or even understand how to do a search on a database? Will they expect a certain level of sophistication on the site, or would they prefer basic text?

- **Can you manage the technology?**

Do you have the resources to edit, maintain and update databases, animations or whatever? Will you have to pay for professional assistance each time you want to add a couple of new facts?

Textual Content in Non-HTML Formats

Acrobat Reader

PDF (portable document format) files are typically used for repurposing or republishing journals, reports and other documents, because they 'fix' the style and layout. This format is perhaps most suitable for documents which are intended for printing, rather than on-screen viewing. In order to view PDF files users must have the free Acrobat Reader plug-in installed on their computer, but this plug-in is now so widespread that few users will be excluded. The full Acrobat program is required to create PDF files, although Photoshop and PageMaker can also export PDF files. Once the full version of Acrobat is installed, you can 'Save as PDF' from most applications, including Word, Excel and others. Links to PDF files should also include a link to allow users to download the Acrobat Reader from Adobe's web site (http://www.adobe.com/products/acrobat/readstep2.html), just in case they do not already have it installed. It is also helpful to tell users the length and file size of PDF documents.

Flash

Some web sites are developed entirely in Flash, with no HTML used at all in the pages. Other sites use Flash simply for one discrete section of the site, to create an interactive game or animated promotional movie, or just for navigation images or banner advert creation. Assuming your users all have Flash installed – and Macromedia claim that this is the case for some 75–80 per cent of browsers – this allows a more dynamic, animated and interactive presentation. However, site content can only be updated by those with Flash development skills and access to the original files – hardly ideal for a multi-contributor environment. As with PDF files, you should provide the option to download the Flash player from the Macromedia web site (http://www.macromedia.com/software/flash/download/). If you are using a Flash animation as an introduction to your site it is important to offer a 'skip intro' option: the animation may be interesting on a first visit, but a sure way to irritate regular visitors is to force them to wait through a 30-second introductory slideshow on each visit. You should also consider providing a full HTML alternative to the content within the Flash movie, for accessibility reasons (see Chapter 4) and for search engine indexing purposes (see Chapter 6).

The guiding principle of web design should be that of usability. The only factor that really counts is whether or not your users can access the information easily, reliably and speedily. Jacob Nielsen, widely regarded as the guru of web usability, defines on his Usability web site (http://www.alertbox.com) several mistakes often made by web designers. While some of these are more a matter of taste and choice, others are simply barriers to the information. The key consideration should be: 'If I remove this (feature, graphic, page) will it damage or reduce the usability of the site?' If the answer is no, then take it out!

Avoiding the Avoidable

The following items are often listed as 'things to avoid at all costs'. But perhaps they should be better regarded as 'things to use only after careful consideration'. There are few absolutes in web design – the only true absolute should be the commitment to the user.

Frames

Although good for aiding navigation on complex sites, frames can cause problems with printing, saving and bookmarking. Badly designed frames can make a site unreadable. Best practice is to keep their use to a minimum, allow scrolling and resizing where necessary, and offer a proper <noframes> alternative.

'If you use frames, consider what each content page will look like if seen without the surrounding frames! Someone might find it via a search engine, bookmark it, or be recommended to it by a friend, rather than seeing it in your intended context. Does it identify your institution? Does it provide a link to the frame set home page?'

Pam Davies
Leeds University Library

Standard Clipart

Despite the millions of graphics available, there are some very recognisable pieces of clipart on web sites: original graphics (or adapted clipart) give a better impression for professional sites – and say something about the designer.

'Under Construction' Signs

A good site should always be under construction! But if it's not ready for viewing, don't publish it. If it genuinely is growing over time then say that, but make it a positive feature, perhaps inviting suggestions and contributions. If you are forced to launch a site (or a section of a site) before it is complete, then make a virtue of its dynamic nature – 'coming soon, information about . . .' – and give a launch date if possible.

Large Files

No visitor ever complained that a page loaded too fast, so optimise graphics where possible to ensure the quickest possible page loading. Large files can be broken in to sections: documents can be divided in to sections of a few pages, and graphics can be 'sliced'. At the very least you should warn users of the size of a large download. Large images could be linked to thumbnail versions on a prior page, so that the user can get an idea of what they selecting. Documents could be offered in different versions – multi-page HTML, a single-page printable version and a PDF file. Software – and most large files – might be better zipped.

> 'Connection speed will vary between users. Always put the file size next to any downloads so that users will have an idea of how much time a download will take.'
>
> **Eddie Stewart**
> **Webmaster, DERA**

Technical Showcases

Advanced features must be sure to enhance the web site, not just the designer's ego. If they are appropriate, expected by the user, if the plug-in is provided or linked, if the audience is capable and interested, then the audience will be in a position to appreciate your efforts. But could that Flash movie, live web cam or 3D walkthrough be presented in a quicker or easier way?

References and Resources

The Safe Colour Cube (http://www.sbu.ac.uk/training/links/cube.html)

Visibone (http://www.visibone.com/colorlab/small.html)

Adobe (http://www.adobe.com)

Macromedia (http://www.macromedia.com)

Site Feature: News Feeds

One of the most interactive elements of any web site is current news. Topical content – changing either daily or, better still, in real time throughout the day – gives the visitor a very powerful reason to return on a regular basis. It also provides you, as the site manager, with great credibility as a source of authoritative information on the topic of your site.

There are three main ways to get news onto your site, as detailed below.

Editorial Team

Employ an editorial team, whose task is to cull news from a range of sources and add it to the web site through the day, or at regular scheduled intervals. This method is effective and credible, because news will be checked for relevance before being added to the site, but expensive in terms of staffing.

News Search Button

Excite, AltaVista, Northern Light and other search engines have in-built news feeds. By performing a search, then saving the URL of the results page and using it to create a button or text link, you have what is effectively a stored search. One click takes you to the current version of that search. This is easy to implement, but the link itself does not change from day to day, and so looks a little static.

- For Excite, replace "keyword" in the URL below with the search term: http://search.excite.com/search.gw?c=timely&sort=date&s=keyword
- For AltaVista, go to http://news.altavista.com and do your search, then save the URL of the results as the link
- NorthernLight news search can be found at http://www.northern-light.com/news.html but only news from press agencies and stories of a certain international status are available.

News Feed

There are now several services, including Moreover and Guardian Unlimited, which enable site managers to add current headlines to their sites. These headlines change constantly through the day and can be on a wide range of topics. The links take you directly to the service's web site for the source of the news, adding high credibility to the originating site.

Guardian Unlimited (http://www.guardianunlimited. co.uk) lets you select from a range of news and editorial topics, including news feeds, specialised content such as business and motoring news, sports news, film news, features and reviews, education news and resources, an archive of *Guardian* and *Observer* articles and the Jobs Unlimited database of job vacancies. This can be done either using a search form that searches a section by keyword, or by harvesting the headlines automatically using a script and inserting them into a preset page on your site. Further information can be found on the *Guardian* web site at http://www.guardianunlimited.co.uk/distribution/

Moreover (http://www.moreover.com) takes news from 1,500 separate sources, and uses over 300 categories to provide free aggregated content in the form of customisable news headlines.

Adding these headlines to your web site is a simple three step process:

1. Select the news feed

2. Click on the 'Webmaster' button at the top of the page

3. After selecting the number of headlines required, copy and paste the resulting code in to your HTML code.

Because Moreover takes the news in as it is produced by the news providers, your visitors can be sure of seeing new and current articles whenever they arrive at your site.

As the Moreover news feed is provided as a large snippet of JavaScript it can be placed anywhere on your page, and using tables can be made to look an integral part of the content.

As well as integrating the news feeds directly into your page, you can also simply place a link to any of the 300+ news topics. One or other of these news solutions provides the beginnings of the creation of a web portal, combining news, links, articles and other specialist resources.

Another service is provided by NewsNow (http://www.newsnowdirect.com) which charges from £95 per month. It allows you to combine a range of news topics into its news feed and specify UK or US news, or both.

Site Feature: Customer Service

Interactivity is essential on a web site, as it provides users with a more interesting and more useful experience, thus reinforcing the customer relationship. Combining interactivity with a customer service function enhances the relationship further. You should provide as many points of contact as possible on a web site, so that the user can have their needs met as easily as possible.

The 'simple' means of customer service contacts are:

- A visible telephone number (not as frequent as it should be!)
- An e-mail link on each page
- A contacts page with full contact details
- An enquiry form for comments, enquiries, complaints, etc.

While these are all excellent and simple to implement, they do require the enquirer to wait for a response, or perhaps to break their Web session to use the telephone.

Here are four other options which add a more professional customer service function to a site. They require a bit more implementation from the web site manager, but the reward is more effective communication with the customer:

They offer quite different approaches, and so are hard to compare directly.

(http://www.realcall.co.uk)

How it works

- Customer clicks on RealCall button
- A pop-up form appears for them to enter their phone number
- The system calls you with their number
- You phone the customer.

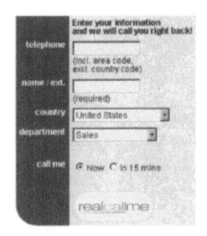

The benefit to the customer is that you pay for the call; the benefit to you is that you get to speak to the customer, explain your services more fully and answer their questions.

Pricing

Starts at 95p per alert received; Enterprise monthly pricing starts at £1,000 set up and £120 per month for up to ten alerts per day.

Features

- Spells out name and extension number
- Reports country of origin
- Can capture extra data about user
- Created easily with HTML wizard
- On-line records for all calls
- Summary and specific records.

(http://www.humanclick.com)

How it works

HumanClick is based on software which is downloaded onto the site manager's (or customer service representative's) PC, combined with the application itself which is hosted by HumanClick. HumanClick is activated whenever you connect to the Internet. By default, the

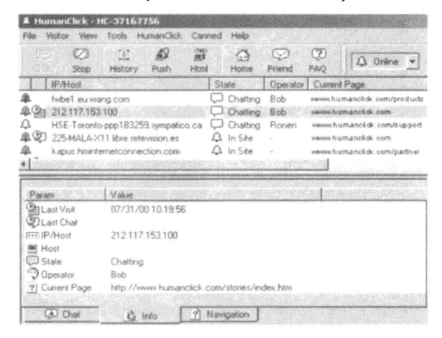

Screen shot showing operator view of HumanClick

HumanClick application is minimized and provides you with an audio/visual alert as visitors browse your site or when they ask to chat with you.

Using the operator window you receive a real-time view of visitors' profiles including information such as their host name, pages viewed, length of visit, etc. At any point during a visit to your site you may, in one click, open a chat request on the visitor's screen and offer assistance.

Pricing
Currently free, HumanClick will shortly become a charged service with an anticipated cost of below $100 per month.

Features

- A database of preset answers can be created·
- A customer's prior history is displayed to the operator
- Operators can run multiple chat sessions simultaneously.

(http://www.claripoint.com)

How it works
During a telephone conversation with a client, subscriber or staff member, you invite them to log on to your Claripoint account – this provides a framed web page, where you can show a PowerPoint presentation, screenshots from any Windows application, or other web pages.

The presentation can be to any number of clients, using a telephone conferencing service for the voice element, as long as they have web access for the visuals.

Pricing
Costs 10p per minute per client for the time that all parties are logged in. No set-up or monthly fees.

Features

- Can be embedded into your web site
- Allows multiple users through teleconferencing
- No software has to be downloaded to watch a presentation.

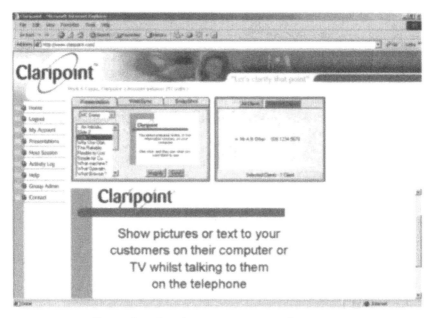

Screenshot showing operator view of Claripoint.

(http://www.liveperson.com)

How it works

LivePerson Chat provides a chat window which is launched when the user clicks on a help button on the web page. Real-time text-based chat enables operators to assist up to four customers at once. The operator can also offer images and links as well as text chat.

Pricing

$2,500 set-up fee, $350 per operator per month.

Features

*   Transcripts, historical tracking and operator performance reports

- No hardware or software to set up
- All services hosted on LivePerson servers
- LivePerson FAQ can act as customer support outside opening hours
- By adding an exit survey following a query, you can collect customer information.

Chapter 4

Site Quality and Accessibility

The practical design and construction processes are just part of the web site mix: testing and validating the site, and running it according to a realistic and ethical set of policies, are as important as elegant design and relevant content.

Testing and Validating

One of the Web's shortcomings as a publishing medium is its lack of a formal editorial process. Anyone can publish anything without external checking. This is excellent for freedom of speech and for universal access to the medium, but it is very limiting in terms of quality control. A quick search on AltaVista for a simple typing error such as 'univeristy' comes up with over 80,000 pages containing the error – and the vast majority of these pages are official institutional pages.

Many sites also have sloppy HTML coding, with broken images, links that don't work, browser incompatibilities and other errors and omissions that demonstrate a poor approach to quality control on the part of the web team – often caused by lack of resources. A web site should reflect favourably on your organisation, deliver a message and present a positive image. Few things undermine customer confidence more effectively than sloppy workmanship.

Establishing and maintaining the technical quality of a web site involves at least five steps:

- Validating the HTML
- Testing the page
- Proof-reading the content
- Testing the instructions
- Testing the back end.

'Check your facts. Spell check. Cut extra words. Then use the tools at sites such as http://www.web-trends.net to get a second opinion.'

Matt Martel
ContentGenerators

Validating the HTML

HTML validation ensures that your code meets the formal standards. This should mean that it appears properly in all versions of the main browsers. One feature of the HTML standard is that older browsers will simply ignore any code that they are not able to understand – this is called graceful degradation, or backward compatibility – which is particularly important if you think that a significant part of your readership might be using older browsers. Most HTML editing software has built-in validation, and if you are hand-coding your pages you could use services such as NetMechanic, Web Site Garage or WebLint.

Testing the Page

Even with perfect HTML, pages can display very differently on a range of equipment: where possible your site should be tested on a PC and a Mac, at different screen resolutions, supporting different numbers of colours, at different screen sizes and using a range of browser versions. At the very minimum you should test your site with Netscape 4 and Explorer 4 and 5 on both a PC and a Mac. Browser emulator software such as Browserola (http://www.codo.com/browserola) can give you an impression of how your page will appear in a range of browsers, highlighting particular issues you might need to design around.

Browser	Percentage of users
MSIE 5.x	64
MSIE 4.x	16
Netscape 4.x	13
Other Netscape	1
Unknown	1
Opera	<1

Source: theCounter.com (http://www.thecounter.com)

As well as testing the look and feel of the site as a whole, you need to check every image and every link on every page. Frequently. The validation tools mentioned above can do this for you, or you can use software such as Linkbot (http://www.linkbot.com) to do this on a scheduled basis.

Proof-reading the Content

For most visitors the content of the site demonstrates your expertise, and spelling and grammatical errors do little to maximise that impression. Get someone else to proof-read articles and features on the site – it is one of the quirks of publishing that it is almost impossible to check your own copy, whereas a passing stranger can take one look and spot errors that have eluded you over several readings.

Testing the Instructions

In the same way that proof-reading your own words is next to impossible, you need to get an external view of how the web site actually operates. You know where each button leads, and what the text on that button means. Invite someone with no knowledge of the web site – perhaps with little

'From developing and managing the Sears Canada web site, I learned you should listen to every crackpot who tells you your site isn't working. Because in over 50 percent of the cases, they are using some combination of technology you never tested with, and they are often right!'

John Pullam
McLean Systems Inc.

experience of the Internet – to try out the site. Can they understand your instructions? Can they find the key parts of the site? Are they confused?

Testing the Back End

If you run your own web server, you need some means of knowing when it's not working – preferably before the customer tells you. And certainly in case the customer *doesn't* tell you. Monitoring software checks that everything is running smoothly, and notifies the appropriate staff should there be a problem.

'Make it as easy as possible for helpful users to report a broken link or other problem with the site offer a 'feedback'' or 'web master'' link from every page, so they don't have to go back to the home page to see how to contact you.'

Pam Davies
Leeds University Library

Services like AtWatch (http://www.atwatch.com) monitor web sites for their customers as often as every five minutes to make sure the site is up, the links work, the site is responsive and the content is there and safe. When it's not, they let you know immediately via pager, fax, e-mail and voice alerts. There is a free version that checks the site every two hours and sends you e-mail alerts. This service can be used for sites hosted on a third-party service. You may not have access to the server to fix it, but you can at least find out how reliable a host's service is over time.

A web site should be a dynamic marketing activity, growing organically through the addition of new content as well as through the development of new areas.

In addition to monitoring the technical performance, there needs to be a constant process of development – or at least of planning – intended to foresee and anticipate the needs of the site's audience several months ahead.

Enable the team contributing to your site to share ideas and deliver content easily: an e-mail discussion list for ideas and to share documents for proof-reading; a form on a private page for the submission of new content; regular meetings to develop strategy and distribute tasks. The web site should not be seen as a discrete project that only has a peripheral relevance to the rest of the organisation. In many cases the web site will be the only part of the organisation that many users see. Your most loyal, profitable customers may only exist as e-mail addresses! The site must be seen as part of the organisation's activities – central to the marketing and development, but also informed and informative on all aspects of internal and external activities and development.

The web team should not be a sprawling committee – changes need to be made promptly, without reference to every single interested party.

Devolved responsibility, specified duties and responsibilities – and specified room for innovation – should keep the site active and lively.

Accessibility

Accessibility in web design provides a high degree of usability for people with disabilities. Mostly based on general design principles, with some specific extra facilities, accessible design ensures that you do not deliver a restricted or exclusionary message – and therefore image. Full accessibility design guidelines are provided by the W3C, the standards body for the Web (http://www.w3.org/WAI).

While the focus of this section is largely on design for blind users who access the web page via a screen-reader, if you make pages accessible in the ways suggested you will improve clarity for all users. The BBC has developed a script called Betsie, which will convert pages to plain HTML. The development of this service is the subject of a case study provided by Betsie's developer, Wayne Myers, on page 107.

There can be a fine line between enabling and excluding technology. All it takes is some careless HTML, the addition of a few unsupported images and some multimedia frills, and entire web sites can disappear from view for substantial numbers of users. Complying with HTML standards, designing for universal access and applying plain English guidelines should be the foundation of any well-designed, content-driven web site, and not just a philanthropic afterthought.

The Disability Discrimination Act 1995 includes requirements for providers of information services – which of course includes web sites – to enable these services for unimpeded access by disabled users. Making your site accessible is not just good practice, or a way of maximising customer service, it is a legal requirement, albeit one that is little enforced as yet.

The HTML design suggestions below are drawn from a variety of sources. Their implementation need not add significantly to the design or management costs of a web site – even less so if they are designed in from the outset. Each adds a little to the universality of the medium. Combined, they can ensure that no users are excluded for reasons of design. The focus is largely on design for blind users who access web pages via a screen-reader. Blind or visually-impaired users are of course not the only people who have difficulty accessing Internet-based information, but the difficulties that this population group experience are probably those most readily resolved by web design. Access solutions for those with learning difficulties and physical mobility problems are mostly centred on support and training, or on hardware and software development, rather than on design of the content.

The suggestions below are based on three basic web design principles: pages should not be browser-specific; they should make sense to all their readers, not just those using particular technologies; images (their description or their meaning within the page) should be accessible to all readers, even those who cannot see them. Universal access to information is a right, not a favour, and designing accordingly is entirely compatible with exciting and attractive web page design.

Technological Solutions

Screen-readers combined with a voice synthesiser (or Braille output), typically using the Lynx text browser, provide access to those with sight or mobility problems. Some screen-readers can work with graphical browsers, but most design advice here and elsewhere is based on the assumption that they are 'reading' Lynx. All graphical browsers provide some customisation facilities, notably the ability to adjust colour, type size and font. Dyslexic or partially sighted users can thus compensate for some poor or problematic designs. Screen magnifiers provide further control over size (and often colour too). Opera (http://www.opera.no) provides a full set of keyboard commands to replace the use of a mouse, as well as a zoom facility to enlarge the screen content up to 1,000 per cent or reduce it to 20 per cent. PwWebSpeak from isSound (http://www.prodworks.com) converts text to speech, supports variable text sizes and allows words in a particular paragraph to be listed and spelled out. It can also provide response to voice commands. A list of enabling technology as well as accessibility design guidelines can be found on the RNIB web site (http://www.rnib.org.uk).

Hypertext in Context

Using 'click here' as a hypertext link is browser specific – Lynx users simply don't click at all and those who control browsers with keyboard commands instead of a mouse are likewise excluded or confused. It is also poor design, as web pages may be printed out, which will render this instruction redundant.

Plain English and Clear Screens

As already stated, there are ways in which end-users can adjust their screen colour, font and text size. However, clear linguistic design – short sentences, clear headings and well-structured content – is the responsibility of the information provider. It is crucial that headers, list items and sentences are ended with proper punctuation, because screen-readers run text on until it is punctuated. They do the same thing after a link, so insert a few spaces in the source code to avoid problems with text losing its meaning. Dates should be presented in universal formats: put August 10th 2000 or 10 August 2000 rather than 10-08-00 or 10/8/00 to prevent confusion in countries that do not conform to the British style of placing the month second.

Images: alt Attribute

HTML provides for an alternative text description to be attached to images in a document. The alt attribute in the <img> tag exists to describe the image, but enables the page designer to explain or clarify the site structure to the user by putting extra information in the alt text for link buttons (alt="news" can be replaced by alt="link to News section"). Text should be short and instructive and should contribute to the page as a whole rather than simply being a long description of an image as this may actually disrupt the flow of the page as it is being read out.

Images Versus Eye-Candy

Illustrations that are purely decorative (eye-candy) should be 'disappeared' by using alt=" ", while images with contextual relevance can be given a useful text alternative. Although you can provide a long, detailed explanation using the alt attribute some browsers will not wrap alt text and may limit how much of it is displayed without scrolling or simply truncate it. Short is therefore best.

Image Maps

Clickable images with multiple links can be problematic to screen-readers: provide a text link to a menu list of the links in the image either on the same page or on a text-only alternative page. If this link disrupts the design of the page consider using an invisible GIF with a useful text description as a link, or even a set of invisible GIFs as an alternative to the image map. Either way the alt statement for the image should be helpful. Client-side image maps allow for alt statements for each coordinate, but an alternative text list – or a link to a text-based page – will be easier for the Lynx screen-reader to translate.

> 'Every web page produced should always contain a text version of the site navigation at the very top. This not only aids navigation visibility and standardisation but is also a valuable tool for users with sensory or motor disabilities. The first option should always be "skip navigation" (with a link down the page) so that users with a disability browser can avoid repetitive commands on each page viewed.'
>
> **Neil Pawley**
> **Consultant, open.gov.uk**

Invisible Links

Create a small, single-colour GIF, say 2 or 3 pixels square, and set the colour as transparent. This image will then be invisible to most readers, and can be used as a 'hidden' link that will only show up in Lynx or if the graphics are turned off. Placed appropriately in the page as a column of unseen links, it can be used to point to text-only pages or provide sets of links that do not intrude on the visual design of the page. This can be particularly useful for image maps or navigation bars, or where you have several links on the same line.

Text Lists

Ordered (numbered) lists, <ol>, are generally more helpful to visually impaired users than unordered lists, <ul>, as the user knows how far down the list they are. In bulleted lists with graphics for the bullet points use alt="1 of 5" and so on to indicate the length of list and the position of the item within that list. Alternatively, graphical bullets can either be commented out (alt=" ") or described as alt="-" or "*". Stating the number of items in the list, perhaps in the title (five reasons why . . . or eight examples of . . .), helps to provide navigational clues that may otherwise be absent.

Lines of Links

Screen-readers cannot cope with multiple links on the same line: where possible a vertical list of links should be used. If an image-bar is an essential part of the design, then perhaps a set of links using vertically arranged invisible GIFs, or a link to a text-only page, may be a solution.

Columns

Columns created using tables or frames cause problems for screen-readers that can only read line-by-line across the screen. Although Lynx manages tables, mostly by inserting a virtual carriage return at the end of each cell, screen-readers simply read across the line, ignoring table cells completely. If the table contents read horizontally – item, then price, then other information – this may be acceptable if each row fits on a single line. However, tables more usually lose their sense completely and are better supported with a complete text alternative.

<font> Attributes

Screen-readers stumble over enlarged or reduced font sizes, particularly if applied to just one letter at the start of a word. The first letter may be simply ignored, seriously limiting the sense of the word or sentence. Proportional sizes, set by heading levels in HTML, are preferable to specified font sizes, as Lynx ignores these due to the limitations of its text-based display.

Punctuation

Screen-readers read out punctuation. Illustrative use of punctuation such as smileys or emoticons – :-) or :-(for example – will be confusing and should be avoided. Abbreviations and acronyms should be spelt out.

Forms and E-Mail Links

Although Lynx supports forms, screen-readers using graphical browsers do not, so a simple e-mail link should be provided for feedback and interaction. It is helpful to mention at the top of the form that the e-mail link is there as an alternative. It is also helpful to state the number of questions or fields in a form.

Frames

The desirability of frames in general is a subject of much debate. Some dislike the waste of screen space, while others welcome the potential improvements to navigability and layout. At the very least, a full <noframes> alternative should be a standard part of any frame-enabled site – simply saying 'Sorry, your browser does not support frames, please download a new browser' is dismissive and lazy.

Redirecting Users

Frequently visitors are themselves expected to find and follow a link to a text-based page. A Perl script that identifies the browser being used by a visitor, and redirects them to a text-based, frame-free page automatically if appropriate, offers an opportunity to present a welcoming feel to a web site.

Java, JavaScript, Shockwave, VRML

'This site is designed for Netscape 4.0+ or Internet Explorer 4.0+' is becoming an increasingly common way for a web designer to proclaim his or her adherence to specific design standards. The latest features may be desirable to the accomplished web designer, but they expect certain levels of equipment, software and even skill from the user. For content-driven sites that focus on public or statutory information it is inappropriate to shut out a proportion of the audience. Sites based on entertainment or marketing may be able to justify only targeting a proportion of their potential audience – or they may simply be missing a potentially lucrative market segment.

The <applet> tag supports alt statements, but make sure they say something more useful than 'You are missing something cool'.

Audio and Video

If video clips are included in a site then some form of captioning must be used. Audio clips should likewise be translated for the benefit of deaf users – as well as for those without multimedia machines.

PDF Files

Although essentially a graphical format, locally held PDF files can be made accessible using Acrobat Access (http://access.adobe.com), a free Windows plug-in which enables screen-readers to access these files. Adobe also provides a free on-line PDF-to-HTML conversion service for PDF files visible on the Internet. This conversion keeps the document's content in reading order, puts it into a single column and preserves any hypertext links. A third option is to use Adobe's proxy web server, which allows seamless conversion of all PDF files, making them readable through the web browser without any need for further action on the part of the reader.

Testing and Validation for Accessibility

There is a version of Lynx (http://www.fdisk.com/doslynx/lynxport.htm) that can be downloaded and run locally on a PC. Alternatively the pages can be tested via Lynx-me, an on-line service which takes a URL and returns the page looking like it would in Lynx (http://ugweb.cs.ualberta. ca/~gerald/lynx-me.cgi). As a general rule, if a page works in Lynx then it is probably accessible. The main exceptions to this are tables, multiple links on a single line and on-line forms. All these may look fine in Lynx but can cause problems for the screen-reader. Fully accessible design involves providing an alternative for each and every one of them – or changing the design itself to be universally accessible. As well as the usual validation to check your HTML coding, you should validate pages on-line with Bobby (http://www.cast.org/bobby), which returns an image of your page with annotations on the points which might offer problems to readers with visual impairment.

A little awareness and some thought are required to design-in accessibility. A complete text alternative is rarely necessary if normal principles of good design are followed. Frequently, efforts to make pages accessible in this way will improve their clarity for all users.

Site Feature: Validation Services

Test, test and test again. This advice is frequently given to web site developers. Checking that the images and links work, checking the instructions within your pages make sense, ensuring that your site is usable – all these are tasks that must not be overlooked if the site is to achieve its objectives. Fortunately there are a number of services on the Web that make this as easy as possible. Here are just a few.

NetMechanic

(http://www.netmechanic.com)

A free validation service that lets you check either one page or 20 pages live through the web site. The test includes a spell check and a link check, image size test, comparison of loading speeds and browser compatibility, as well as HTML validation and <meta> tag checking.

The results are presented in clear tabular form, and the HTML validation shows the code with the errors and corrections highlighted in red, with links to more detailed explanations of the errors in question. A $35.00 subscription lets you check 100 pages within a single URL for a year, with regular scheduled tests and e-mail notification of results.

W3C
(http://validator.w3.org)

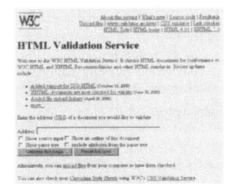

The W3C is the standards body for the Web, and their HTML validator provides validation up to the latest versions of HTML, XHTML and ISO-HTML, as well as checking how well formed the XML is. You can batch upload files for checking and set several variables for the testing.

Bobby

(http://www.cast.org/bobby)

Bobby is a web-based tool that analyses Web pages for their accessibility to people with disabilities. The web site offers a free page check, or you can download the free Bobby validation software and test your whole site. This services checks for compatibility with the W3C accessibility guidelines, and sites that meet the validation criteria are entitled to use the 'Bobby approved' logo to demonstrate the site's commitment to accessibility.

Browser Emulators

Emulation software allows you to see how your site would look in a different format or on a different platform. With WAP and WebTV formats becoming more widely used it is crucial to at least have an idea as to whether your site is at all visible, or whether you can provide specific pages for format-dependent viewers. These services offer a means to check an existing web page in the chosen format before going to the effort of redesigning it.

Lynx and Browserola both provide a means to ensure that your site achieves an acceptable level of backward compatibility, something that is of particular importance if a significant section of your readership is using older browsers.

WAP (http://www.gelon.net)

WebTV (http://developer.webtv.net/design/tools/viewer/)

Lynx (http://www.delorie.com/web/lynxview.html)
> A web view of your page in a text browser, which will give a good idea of how visually impaired users would hear your page through a voice synthesiser:

Browserola (http://www.codo.com/browserola/)
> Downloadable software that presents a page in Netscape 1.2, 2, 3 or 4 and Explorer 2, 3 or 4 among other formats.

Adobe Access
(http://access.adobe.com)

The PDF format provides a useful means for publishing documents on to the Web, but as PDF is essentially a graphic format screen-readers cannot covert the page to speech.

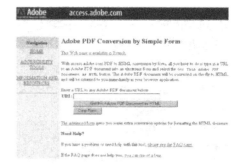

Adobe provides tools to assist visually impaired users: an

accessible page providing advice on how to download and install the Acrobat Reader, and a converter to change a PDF file into a plain text file to enable you to offer a simple alternative on your site. This can be done through a web-based form, or through e-mail submission.

Case Studies 2

BBC Betsie

Dotgain

Motley Fool

OUT-LAW.COM

National Gallery

This second group of case studies includes a wide range of experiences, from in-house developers to professional design services fulfilling clients' briefs. The BBC case study in particular underlines the concept of 'generous design', with a service created for a very specific purpose released for the benefit of the whole community. Communities are a theme in several studies, whether in 'Foolish' discussions about investment or in the membership organisations earlier in the book. Quality and continuity issues are another important topic, with examples in the areas of technical design, discussion board management and supervision, news and feature content as well as optimised image files.

Links to the web sites and services featured in the case studies and throughout this book can be found on the supporting web site, http://www.webtipsandtricks.co.uk

BBC Betsie

(*http://www.bbc.co.uk/education/betsie*)

Betsie stands for BBC Education Text to Speech Internet Enhancer, and is a CGI script written in Perl, designed to alleviate some of the problems experienced by blind or visually impaired web users.

As the BBC version of Betsie is restricted to BBC sites an open source version has also been released, and a number of other sites have customised Betsie to enhance their own accessibility.

Betsie was developed and is maintained by Wayne Myers, a software engineer and a member of the BBC Digital Media technical team.

Details: written in Perl; Betsie means no frames, JavaScript, Java, Flash, audio/video or animations
Server software: Apache
Team: one person
Design: in-house
History: launched December 1998; latest version released September 2000
Monthly visits: approx. 400,000
Usability: optimised for full accessibility

By Wayne Myers (Software Engineer, BBC Digital Media)

Introduction and Background

The Betsie project originated as a response to a serious complaint about the inaccessibility of the BBC site. In the spring of 1998, the BBC web site was, like a lot of sites, designed in such a way as to be almost entirely inaccessible to blind or visually impaired users. When the RNIB (Royal National Institute for the Blind) pointed this out to the BBC, a meeting was arranged to sort the problem out.

During the meeting the RNIB people sat there describing many detailed and specific HTML problems, while the BBC people, myself included, nodded awkwardly, avoided eye contact, and generally shifted around uncomfortably in our chairs. However, towards the end of the meeting I realised that many of the problems could be fixed automatically by a CGI filter script, so I asked if anyone had done this before. When I heard that the answer was 'no' I went off and had a go at doing it myself, and by the following weekend I had a working 'first draft' of what was to become Betsie.

Despite the best efforts of the W3C (World Wide Web Consortium), the vast majority of web sites out there still have major accessibility problems. These problems can be divided into two categories: those that are the result of poor editorial strategies, and those that are the result of poor coding strategies.

Problems in the first category – such as poorly written (or unwritten) alt text for images – cannot easily be fixed by software. Although interesting experiments in this area have been carried out, the fact is that human intervention is required to solve the vast majority of editorial problems. Problems in the second category, however, can often be solved using software – although it does depend on just how poor the code involved is. One example of this type of problem is the prevalent usage of columnar design in web pages, as if the Web were some kind of DTP-like medium. Such designs are typically handled badly by the access software used by the blind and visually impaired community.

Using a text-only browser or a decolumnising browser does not necessarily help much, since the same long, left-hand navigation list tends to appear at the top of every page, which makes it hard to know whether or not a new page is in fact the one that you wanted. A server-side filter transform tool can be used instead, to ensure that when a page is 'decolumnised' the standard navigation elements appear at the bottom instead of at the top, resulting in an on-the-fly text-only version of the site that is actually navigable by users. The alert reader will already have guessed that Betsie is, in fact, just such a tool.

Issues, Solutions and Outcomes

Once I had my list of specific issues raised by the RNIB, and I had figured out the basics of implementing a CGI filter script in Perl, all that remained was to work out which of those issues could be solved using Perl and which would require direct human intervention.

It turned out that decolumnisation was a fairly simple matter of identifying the standard left-hand navigation bar (on the BBC site), moving it to the bottom of the page, and then removing all table tags. This produced a result not unlike that of decolumnising text-only browsers such as Lynx, but that was more practically useful. However, if a page had been designed such that the tables in it did not degrade gracefully there was little that Betsie could do about the resulting mess.

Additionally, while it was a fairly simple matter to remove all image tags and replace them with their alt text, not much could be done about the fact that in many cases – I would go so far as to say more often than not –

the alt text was either not supplied or was not consistent with the high editorial standards demanded by the BBC.

I struggled for a long time to make Betsie work with JavaScript. However, since much of the JavaScript on the BBC site made all manner of erroneous assumptions about things like how many images were on the page (none, after being parsed by Betsie), and much of it was also syntactically dubious anyway, I decided to have Betsie remove all JavaScript. It is possible that a future version may someday only remove the JavaScript that would be broken by the Betsie transforms, but I can't see how to parse arbitrary code for this.

No matter how hard I tried to make Betsie be lenient about invalid HTML, some pages would simply make Betsie hang when she tried to parse them. The sensible solution seemed to be to demand that the BBC stop posting web pages that were not valid HTML – this was something that we (and, indeed, any organisation) ought to have been doing anyway.

Betsie was in fact ready for release by the autumn of 1998, but the release was delayed until the site had caught up with what became known internally (and rather ponderously) as 'Betsie Compliance'. All pages had to be valid HTML, all images had to have alt attributes of a suitable editorial standard (even though in practice, alt="" was and is often the best solution) and all tables had to degrade gracefully.

However, a consequence of this process was that awareness of accessibility issues was forced upon not just myself, but all site producers, designers and coders. The very existence of accessibility issues often comes as news even to experienced web professionals, so the overall educative impact of the internal implementation of Betsie was positive and ongoing – albeit imperfect, to the extent that there remains a small percentage of pages on the BBC site that even Betsie can't do much with.

Finally, although the Betsie code could in theory deal with arbitrary web sites, the operational fact of the matter is that you operate an anonymised browsing service (where the site being converted would log the visitor as the BBC, rather than the individual requesting the page through Betsie, essentially allowing untraceable access to the site) either intentionally or at your peril. Neither of these options constitutes any part of the BBC's on-line remit at this time, so code was included in Betsie to block access to sites outside of the bbc.co.uk domain. The main consequence of this was that I was given permission to place Betsie under an open source licence, and distribute the code freely such that other sites could use it – you can find out more about this on the Betsie site.

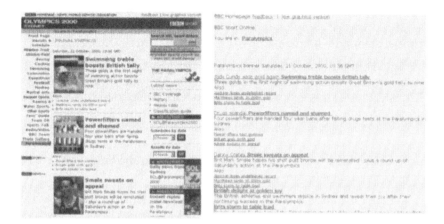

Example BBC web page before and after using Betsie text-only option.

Critique of Solutions

There have been various issues with Betsie, both now and in the past.

The original release of Betsie removed all coloration from the page. However, this meant that colours reverted to whatever the default browser settings were, and I received a number of e-mails from people complaining about this. My solution was to make Betsie enforce her own colour scheme, and after consulting informally with various people I found that research has shown that yellow on a black background is widely considered to be the easiest combination to read.

However, this is a highly subjective thing, and after a day in which I received one e-mail from a visually impaired user congratulating me on choosing such clear, easy-to-read colours, and one e-mail from another user berating me for choosing such a hard-to-read colour scheme in what was supposed to be accessibility software, I implemented a settings system so that users can choose their own colour scheme and stop bothering me with e-mail messages on the subject. The settings page currently allows you to set the font size from very small to very large, since different visual impairments require different solutions – for example, very large fonts are not suitable for impairments that result in perfect eyesight over a highly restricted field of view. You can also set it up so that all web pages look like Windows error messages, but this is more by way of being my little joke, and I don't believe anyone has actually used that feature.

As it happens, by this stage I was beginning to receive e-mail messages from people using Betsie who were neither blind nor visually impaired, but simply preferred the text-only view of the BBC site. It took us all some time to realise that this is exactly what Betsie is – a text-only 'viewifier'. Text-only pages download much more quickly, and cannot hide poorly written content in a welter of flashy design. Text-only pages are not useful just for blind or visually impaired users, but for any context in which you want the information – just the information, nothing but the information, and no pretty pictures or logos to go with it. People with slow connections, older browsers, or hand-held Internet-connected devices tend to find that the Betsie version of the BBC site is more suitable for them than the original. This is a side-effect of the overriding goal of accessibility, so while it may not be true that the Betsie project has actually killed a lot of birds with one stone, it would appear to have seriously injured a few, and only time will tell what direction things will take in terms of the uptake of text-only browsing technology.

Like any software solution, bugs and operational difficulties are inevitable. Without a budget it was not possible to implement any kind of large-scale user testing or anything like that – this problem, bluntly, was counter-balanced by the public release of the Betsie source code. Because the code is now open source, many bugs and operational issues have been picked up by helpful people and better coders than me around the world. I am incredibly grateful to these people, and the quality of Betsie has improved dramatically as a result. This improvement is an ongoing process, and I am sure that a number of (minor) bugs remain to be fixed, but the very worst of my original errors have now been removed. (I hope!)

Betsie was one of the first major Perl projects I had taken on, and various parts of the code are long overdue for a complete rewrite. Version II has been in development for some time now, and I am hopeful that it will be released eventually. But what is out there works, and does the job, so this is really nothing more than a fairly minor issue too.

The really major issue is that Betsie runs the risk of insulating designers, producers and coders from the need to properly learn about accessibility issues, by giving them a false sense of security and making them think that they don't need to worry about such things because Betsie solves all their problems for them. Although this is not the case it is unwise to underestimate the capacity of people to misunderstand things, and I have been fairly robust about constantly reminding people that Betsie is a repair tool rather than an excuse to continue writing inaccessible code. Nevertheless, people have continued writing inaccessible code anyway, and I do believe that to an extent the Betsie-as-excuse trap has been fallen into.

My answer now is more on the practical level – it may well be the case that people use Betsie as a crutch and as an excuse, but the practical upshot is that 'Betsified' sites are more accessible than they otherwise would be. Fortunately I am not blind, but if I were I would rather be able to get some level of access to a site via imperfect means, such as Betsie, than no access at all, as is effectively still the case with an alarmingly large number of web sites. Betsie is a practical, real-world tool, and those with a bent for academic purism tend to recognise her for the basically hackish entity she is, and, quite correctly, run miles.

Through the good work of the W3C Betsie will hopefully be obsolete in a few years. Until such time as the web has evolved to a state where the underlying code makes it impossible for people to code inaccessible sites, however, there will be a need for Betsie or tools like her.

Resources

For more information, source code, a free license and installation instructions, visit the Betsie web site at: http://www.bbc.co.uk/education/betsie/

For a good starting point on accessibility issues in general, visit the W3C Web Accessibility Initiative site at: http://www.w3.org/WAI/

Dotgain

(http://www.dotgain.co.uk)

The Dotgain site is an e-commerce web portal. It supports the book publishing community and allows printers and publishers to efficiently exchange quotes. It was created because we at Texonet saw a unique opportunity to reuse the technologies we had already developed for our engineering customers. In both cases the key to successful execution was a deep understanding of data storage and scalable user access.

The following study is taken from the internal documentation we used to develop and review our product development policy. We share it here in the hope that our experiences will help inform you, the reader, as to the types of issues to consider when developing a web site. The issues we present here are by no means exhaustive, and because of the space limitations we have presented just the key points that we consider crucial in maintaining a high-quality product. These principles were first applied to the Dotgain site and continue to be applied to our current projects.

By Paul James (Technical Director, Texonet)

Frames: no	JavaScript: yes	Java: no
Flash: no	Audio/video: no	Animation: no
HTML editor: Texonet internal editor		
Database: MySQL		
FTP: n/a	Graphics: Paint Shop Pro 6	
Server software: Cobalt RaQ running Apache and PHP version 3		
Team: four people		
Design: outsourced		
History: launched April 2000		
Usability: minimum specification (i.e. 640 × 480, 256 colours), Internet Explorer 3 or Netscape 3		

Texonet Ltd was formed in 1998 to deliver Internet solutions to the engineering industry, and was successful in providing intranet-based infrastructure to blue-chip companies such as BG Transco. The infrastructure we developed allowed our customers to take information from a diverse set of sources and build a coherent view of their business process. We were able to deliver this view through multiple distribution channels, such as the Web, e-mail, WAP and voice.

While developing our intranet systems we gained a great deal of knowledge of providing efficient, reliable, and secure web-based applications. At the beginning of 2000 we felt that it would be appropriate to reapply the techniques and core technologies to a wider market. For this reason Texonet partnered with Dotgain to produce a business-to-business (B2B) site. Dotgain.co.uk aims to be the definitive source of information and services for anyone who makes book publishing happen. It provides an on-line quotation service, plus news, reviews and details of vacancies in the book trade.

Texonet Ltd wanted to continue to commercialise the knowledge gained and has spun off a company called txnt.com to develop the key technologies and push these into new markets. Our development environment now allows data publication through multiple platforms such as the Web, WAP, iMode, WebTV and the Palm Pilot, and in multiple formats such as HTML, WML, CHTML, PDF, Flash and a variety of flavours of XML.

Our first commercial venture using the development platform was webparc.com. This is an Internet business that will provide web-based products to help small- and medium-sized companies to enhance their own Internet presence.

Maintaining Hosting Quality

Whether you are installing your own hardware or outsourcing your installation to a third-party hosting service there are certain key issues that need to be addressed. With the Dotgain contract, as with our current Internet clients, we suggested a third-party solution. Hosting a single site is an expensive proposition, requiring a company to build infrastructure and take on dedicated staff. Hosting service companies are able to fulfil most requirements for a considerable reduction in cost.

When looking at a hosting solution it is usual to concentrate on the software and service packages offered. These packages are usually a mix of services, with a physical resource allocation (disk space) and network resource allocation (bandwidth). However, when choosing a hosting service it is also important to review the security measures in place and the quality of service offered.

Alternative Paths

Hosting services hook onto the Internet to provide connectivity for your server. If their connection were to go down then your server would be out of action. It is therefore imperative that your hosting service has multiple routes to the Internet, and in fact most hosting services have at least three alternative connections. (We specify three as a minimum requirement for our clients.)

Uninterruptible Power Supply
An uninterruptable power supply (UPS) is also important for a high-quality site. A UPS is a backup power supply that kicks in if the main power supply is interrupted. This is important not only to maintain the uptime of your server, but also to allow graceful shutdowns. A graceful shutdown is the process of allowing the machine to cleanly shut down its internal resources. If power is suddenly removed from a server then there is a probability of corruption in the system or, worse, in the database. For this reason a UPS is an essential requirement to protect your web site.

Fire and Flood Detection
The hosting services that we suggest to our clients always have support for fire and flood detection and suppression. Servers sit in unmanned rooms, and it is important that in the event of fire (or flood) an automated system protects your web server.

Secure Location
Of course all of these issues mean nothing if somebody can walk into the hosts' building and walk off with your server. As part of the service the hosting company should provide an adequate level of security.

Quality of Support
Finally, the differences between hosting services are narrowing all the time. In fact, the only way to really differentiate between them in the current market is by the quality of their customer support. It is always worth checking the level of support available and seeing how it fits with your own requirements.

The Dotgain Hosting Solution
Texonet Ltd not only builds web sites for its customers, it also provide a continual maintenance and support service. In the case of Dotgain Ltd this allows them to concentrate on selling trading accounts while we concentrate on providing their web service.

For Dotgain we chose a hosting service using the criteria outlined above. In addition, we reduced the possible impact of relying on a third-party support service by co-locating our client's servers. This means that we provided a server that is installed on the host's network and we manage this server in its entirety. The only services we require from the host are Internet connectivity and infrastructure such as the domain name service (DNS). (This identifies to the domain name registry the physical location of the data identified by the URL.) In addition, the hosting service carries out a full server back-up once a week. This is in addition to our own daily internal back-up procedures.

Selecting your Hardware and Software

Architecture Scalability
The site must be able to handle the expected traffic. If your projections show a growth in the traffic then both your software and hardware should be able to cope with this growth. You may need to take into account support for multiple web servers and/or multiple database servers. This will of course increase your requirements for support and maintenance.

We continually monitor the traffic flows through our clients' servers. From experience it is prudent to plan for expected traffic at least six months in advance. To provide the level of scalability required we use a mix of operating systems (Linux, Sun Solaris, Microsoft NT) and server software (Apache, Internet Information Server, Microsoft Exchange, Microsoft SQL Server, Postgres, MySQL, Oracle).

In the case of the Dotgain site the projected traffic was low, as the total market size is some 1,500 users. We currently rely on a single Cobalt RaQ to provide all of the services for the Dotgain site. This set-up is more than capable of handling the current site requirements.

Developing your Scripts

The core technology to your site is the back-end scripting. Once you have secured your platform, and written your code, then the single most important function you can carry out is testing. There are two main reasons for exhaustively testing your implementation: script errors and security holes.

Script Errors
The first reason for testing is to pick up errors in scripts. If a script fails it generally outputs a message to the browser that is designed to help the programmer with debugging. If a fatal error occurs, for example a connection to the database can't be made, the script should fail elegantly.

Warning: SQL error: [Microsoft][ODBC Driver Manager] Data source name not found and no default driver specified, SQL state IM002 in SQLConnect in D:\Webparc\html\index.php3 on line 9

Standard error messages give the user too much information.

User Notification

There has been a problem with this service and we are
unable to log you on at this time. Our support staff have
been notified and will contact you if required. Please try
again later.

Support Phone Number: ???? ??? ????
Please quote reference [032234]

User-oriented error messages are 'friendlier'.

In other words, a user-oriented message should be displayed. This is not
only more helpful to your customer but it makes your site more secure.
The debug information that is usually dumped is there to tell the
programmer as much about the error as possible. It could of course be
used to uncover information about how the site was constructed and
may even allow access to your scripts.

Execution Holes

Execution holes can introduce the most dangerous security breaches in
your system. If your scripts execute external programs or run database
queries then there is an opportunity for an execution hole. For example,
a particular script may take a parameter from an HTML form and insert
it into a database query. If insufficient checking is done on the input
parameter the user can insert anything into the query, including an
instruction to delete entries from the table or reveal account passwords.

This concept carries over to the execution of external programs: if an
input parameter is passed as a command line parameter this could allow
an end user to directly execute programs on your server.

If you use JavaScript to validate form data then you must still validate
the data on the server scripts. Even if the JavaScript catches all the
execution holes the user may have JavaScript turned off, and it is
important to remember that it is simple to construct a page that pushes
unchecked data to the server.

Developing the Dotgain Site

We tested the Dotgain site extensively, in conjunction with Dotgain Ltd.
As part of our development strategy we run three separate versions of
the site: the first is our own internal development site, where our
programmers and designers can develop new services; the second is a
beta site, which can be accessed by the Dotgain staff and a group of beta
users who are helpful in uncovering site errors and suggesting
enhancements to the service; and the final version is of course the live
site where the Dotgain trading floor is hosted.

Conclusion

We have seen many web design houses use cost alone as the key driver for site development. A web site is slowly becoming a prime source of company information and, with services like our own webparc.com, an important interaction space for a company's suppliers, customers and personnel.

Our company is not a pure design house but is also a software development house. We are keen to bring the same diligence to our web services that we do to our engineering customers. The quality of web services and sites available is currently very low. It is amazing to see unforgivable mistakes being made by the big brand sites, either through an inability to scale to their traffic or through basic development practices.

The key to developing a quality web service is testing. This testing is not limited to the code development process but includes a continual evaluation of requirements against the fulfilment options. A web site is not only an extension of a company's brand, but is also a product in itself. The quality of the site reflects directly back onto the company, and a badly constructed web site is one of the quickest ways to lose a customer. In conclusion, we include a series of checklists of the key points introduced here.

Hosting Service Checklist
- Redundant Internet routes – make sure the hosting service supports multiple Internet routes
- Uninterruptible power supplies – make sure your server(s) can survive a power outage
- Fire and flood detection and suppression – make sure your server(s) can survive a fire or flood
- Secure physical installation – make sure your server(s) can't be stolen
- Quality support service – make sure you get the level of service you require
- Automated backup – make sure your data is backed up regularly.

Hardware/Software Checklist
- Hardware/software scalability – make sure you can handle projected traffic (six months lead time).

Script Development Checklist
- Elegant script failure – make sure all errors fail with a user-friendly message and don't display sensitive configuration information
- Look for execution holes in your site scripts – make sure all the input data is properly validated before insertion into SQL statements or program parameters.

The Motley Fool UK

(http://www.fool.co.uk)

The Motley Fool web site is named after a character from Shakespeare's *As You Like It*. It approaches the normally dry world of personal finance and investing with the spirit of the Fool behind the web site being embodied in the words of the Bard when he says:

'Invest me in my motley; give me leave
To speak my mind, and I will through
 and through
Cleanse the foul body of th' infected
world, ...'

While the editorial side of the web site brings a fresh approach to finance, the discussion boards serve a community of readers, providing a forum for them to share information and insight, to learn from and teach each other.

By George Row (Community Producer, Motley Fool UK)

Frames: No	JavaScript: Yes	Java: No
Flash: No	Audio/video: No	Animation: Only in advertising
Software: message board software developed in-house		
Team: ten people		
Design: in-house		
History: UK site launched February 1998		
Monthly page views: 12 million page views, 50,000 messages		
Site size: 5,000 pages of static content; 1 million messages		
Usability: version 3 and above of Netscape and Internet Explorer		

Introduction – Who is this Fool?

I sat down to write this case study with just a hint of a hangover, having attended a party the previous night for the London-based readers of The Motley Fool. The party was organised by the readers through the social events discussion board of the web site (http://boards.fool.co.uk/Messages.asp?bid=50929). Many of those attending had never met before – at least not face-to-face. There was a collection of people of all ages and backgrounds, ranging from a young woman just out of college to a recently retired director of a public company, from a designer of integrated circuits to a journalist, through to people whose only contact with either chips or newspapers would be at the take-away on the way home. I was surrounded by people who were shaking hands and exclaiming things like: 'CrazyRabbit? I didn't expect you to look like this!' The one thing that all these people had in common was our web site, where they gather daily to share information and knowledge and offer each other insight and support. Having worked with computers, networks and people for the last 25 years I have been privileged to have had quite a few of the 'Wow!' experiences which the Internet serves up, but meeting all these people last night was particularly special.

We humans are social animals. Much of our emotion and intuition, our problem solving and intelligence, comes from interacting with others, sharing information, trying out ideas, gaining confidence and learning new ways of approaching a problem. All of us who turn to the Internet as our first source of information have had the experience of a family member or a friend raising a sceptical eyebrow as we go on-line in response to a problem. Typically they will tell us to 'Switch off the computer and talk to real people instead of that machine!' On hearing this sort of thing we know that we are dealing with someone for whom the Internet experience has not yet 'clicked'. The computer is important as an information-processing machine, but it is when it is combined with real people that its potential to change the world is unleashed.

The real power of the Internet, then, is as a tool for computer-mediated communication (CMC) between people. There is in fact a quarterly journal – *Journal of Computer-Mediated Communication* – dedicated to the study of CMC, which has been available on the Web since June 1995 (http://www.ascusc.org/jcmc/). Over the three years since we launched The Motley Fool UK we have aimed to give the site a sense of place. We have striven to make it a friendly, welcoming place, where it is rewarding to share what you know and safe to admit what you don't know. The discussion boards have lived up to our expectations that they would be used to discuss bargains in car insurance, to explain how to calculate the annual return on an investment and to share information about, and preferences for, investments in the stock market. However, we have also seen those discussion boards used to make friends, found investment clubs and organise parties. They have become a source of support for members going through difficult times – for a time one of our boards was the point of rendezvous for insomniac parents whose babies had woken in the night. For many of our regular posters the message boards have become the place where they boast of their triumphs and where they turn for support in times of disaster. Meanwhile, for the lurkers (the ones who read but never post) all this is played out before them like a real-life soap opera that they can watch and from which they can learn.

Issues and Themes in Community-Based Web Sites

The potential of communities based on CMC has been recognised by a wide spectrum of people over recent years. These have ranged from idealists like Howard Rheingold of the WELL (the original counter-culture community web site) to business consultants such as Hagel and Armstrong. Rheingold's book *The Virtual Community* (1993) looked at how electronic communities could contribute to culture and democracy, while Hagel and Armstrong's *Net Gain* (1997) considered their potential for commercial exploitation. As a web site with a mission to make a business out of putting the individual in charge of his or her finances, our experiences at The Motley Fool have touched on many points along this spectrum.

Throughout the 1990s awareness spread of early virtual communities such as the WELL (Rheingold, 1993; Figallo, 1998). In the early 1990s new virtual communities were created, such as the New York Cyberpunk site called MindVox, which was founded in 1990. At first simply a community site, MindVox diversified to become an early public ISP and finally went out of service in 1997 as the ISP sector became more competitive (Cavanaugh, 1996; Alderman, 1997).

In a web search carried out while preparing his book, Cliff Figallo (1998) found that towards the end of 1997 there were thousands of matches for a search on the phrase 'on-line community'. When I repeated this search three years later I found hundreds of thousands of matches via AltaVista and Excite, and millions of matches on Google and Lycos. Hagel and Armstrong (1997) addressed the opportunities for commercial exploitation. However, amongst the proliferation of web sites claiming to include a virtual community are many which reflect a mistaken view that simply bolting message board software on to a web site is the same as building a community – it is not. Some of the early idealists (Figallo, 1998) view this as a superficial response to Hagel and Armstrong's analysis.

Bolting general tools together will not give your users 'a sense of place'. It is important that the tools for interaction form an integrated whole with a coherent look and feel. We have discussed this in the context of educational CMC systems (McDaid *et al.*, 1999) and it applies equally to community systems. A group identity is, if anything, more important than the technology and the sense of place.

A community depends on the commitment and loyalty of its members, and this does not come from technology alone. A discussion board has the potential to become a community in the same way that a vacant piece of land has the potential to become a garden. They both need care and feeding, nurture and weeding. As Rheingold (1993) puts it:

> 'When you think of a title for a book, you are forced to think of something short and evocative, like, well, "The Virtual Community",

even though a more accurate title might be: "People who use computers to communicate, form friendships that sometimes form the basis of communities, but you have to be careful to not mistake the tool for the task and think that just writing words on a screen is the same thing as real community".'

So if you are developing a community aspect to your web site, why should the casual web surfer visit your site in preference to the many alternatives? Hagel and Armstrong (1997) were convinced of the commercial potential of the community-based web site. They were also clear about the prerequisites to unlock that power:

'Virtual communities have the potential to drive a major shift in power from vendor to customer ... to aggregate purchasing power by providing a compelling environment that draws in new members . . . This ... is helped enormously by the first defining characteristic of a virtual community: a distinctive focus as to membership.'

To achieve a distinctive focus not only do you need to have a clear idea of your aim in having a community aspect to your site, this aim also needs to be something which can be communicated to the potential users and with which they can identify. If you can find a slogan which epitomises your goals, all the better. On The Motley Fool web site we have a tag line 'To Educate, Amuse and Enrich'; this appears throughout the site and expresses our overall aim. We also have a community slogan, 'Civil Discussion for Mutual Benefit', which is often invoked on our discussion boards to define the ethos that we are trying to achieve.

Once you have established the focus, what makes a community gather around that focus? Cliff Figallo (1998) identified what he sees as the attributes of an on-line community which solidify loyalty to the group and therefore to the site that supports it:

- 'The member feels part of a larger social whole
- There is an interwoven web of relationships between members
- There is an exchange between members of commonly valued things
- Relationships between members last through time, creating shared history.'

Amy Jo Kim (2000) emphasised the membership life cycle of a community. For her it is important that the web site management does each of the following: welcome visitors, instruct novices, reward regulars, empower leaders, honour elders. In the rest of this article we will look at how we address many of these issues on The Motley Fool site.

In my view, from the start of the design process you have to consider these questions about the members of your community:

- Who are these people?
- What will they get from your community?
- Why have they come to your web site?
- Why do you want them to come to your web site?
- What are they going to talk about?

In the case of The Motley Fool we have the editorial side of the web site. It sets a tone. It defines us as being on the side of the individual investor. We have a sub-text throughout the site (and our books) of putting individuals in charge of their destiny.

A Description of the Fool Discussion Boards System

Our discussion boards are organised into a fairly flat hierarchy of folders. At the top level they are divided into eleven themed folders, as shown on the left of the screen-shot in Figure 1. There are about 1,000

Figure 1: The front page of The Motley Fool discussion boards.

separate discussion boards on which approaching a million messages have been posted over the last three years. We provide facilities for users to request and suggest new discussion boards. The route to content is via a message board view, such as the one shown in Figure 2.

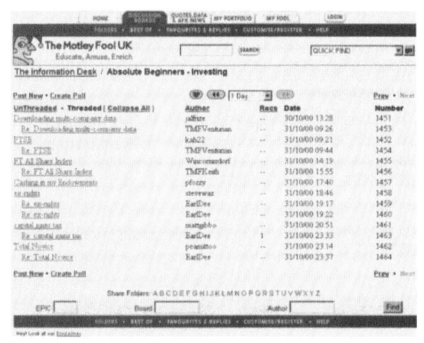

Figure 2. The board view page, showing the
message subjects and thread structure.

Reading the Fools' Discussion
The front page of the discussion boards area (http://boards.fool.co.uk) acts as the top level of the folder structure, as shown in Figure 1. Each board is dedicated to a particular area of discussion. Within a board's subject area any user may start a discussion on a new topic. The messages making up one particular conversation on a particular topic are referred to as a 'thread'. The boards are mostly on financial and investing topics; over half of them in the 'Shares A–Z' area have as their topic a single company, and are aimed at the shareholders of that particular company. Having gathered a community of individuals numbering hundreds of thousands we have found that they do occasionally want to talk about things other than money, and increasingly we have added boards on other topics.

The links on the left of the boards' front page allow readers to start their navigation through the folder hierarchy to select the discussion board in which they are most interested. The links on the right provide shortcuts to common starting points along with links to static pages such as the posting guidelines. When users reach a board they are first shown the board view page (Figure 2). This lists the subject and author for each message, the date and time of the message and the number of times it has been recommended by other readers. The links at the top of the columns allow the view to be changed. The reader can choose to see the messages organised in any of these styles:

- by thread – for following a particular discussion
- by date – to keep track of the latest messages
- by author – to follow the contributions of particular person
- by recommendation – to pick out only the best content.

There is a design principle at work here – provide multiple views and let the user choose the one that suits.

A popular message board will quickly fill up with thousands of messages. Providing access to a discussion archive is one way of reducing the tendency of new users to bring up the same old topics, which will have already been exhaustively discussed by the regulars. The Fool system also provides mechanisms for searching and skipping through the messages.

When users find a topic that looks interesting they can click on the subject line to display the message (see Figure 3). There is a lot in this window besides the text of the message, and later we'll come back to some of the interactive features. For now, lets just try to 'read' this message display page.

The person posting this message has quoted a question from a previous message in italic before giving his answer. The name of the author of the message is at the top left; the star symbol after his name is added by the system as an indicator of the total number of messages he has posted. The number of recommendations (at the top right) shows that two other readers liked it when they read it. Remember that on the discussion board view page it was possible to organise the messages by recommendations? That feature is driven by this number, and can be invaluable for catching up on activity on a board – it allows you to read the most popular messages first, and then perhaps follow into discussions of interest.

Above the text of the message is the subject of the current thread, the name of the board on which it appears and the name of the 'frequently asked questions' (FAQ) message for this board. Each of these is itself a link. The subject link takes us to the message to which this is a reply, and the message board name link takes us to the board view page showing

Figure 3. Reading a message on The Motley Fool discussion boards.

the overall structure of the dialogue. The FAQ link goes to a message answering the most frequently asked questions. The heart symbol refers to the discussion board rather than the author. To make a board a favourite, users simply click on the heart: a 'favourite boards' page will then keep them up-to-date on activity on those boards. When regular readers log on to the Fool site they are shown their favourite boards page as a starting place, and this provides a short cut to the discussions that interest them.

Contributing to the Discussion
The message posting page (Figure 4) is the first feature that someone has to master to become a full participant in the discussion. Another of our

---

Original Message   Subject: Re: Dividend/results timing
                   Author: DaveWuzz   Date: 26/9/00 09:30   Number: 1307

One last question: how does the ex-div date relate to the results dates?

The ex-div date is the first day on which shares are traded without entitlement to
dividend. Up to that date sellers transfer to buyers the rights to whatever dividend
said in my last post, the market will factor this into the price. After the ex-div date
not the buyer who is entitled to the dividend.

I don't believe there is any sort of generally applicable timescale. The dividend is
always, paid around the anniversary of the equivalent preceding dividend and the
usually be perhaps 5 or 6 weeks ahead of that. But all these dates are determined
company and announced to the market in due course.

(Using your mouse you can highlight, copy, and then paste any of the above message

Your Reply

Subject: Re: Dividend/results timing
Author: TMFGrow

[Submit Reply]   [Preview Reply]   [Cancel Reply]

Figure 4. Posting a message on The Motley Fool discussion boards.

community design principles – we want good quality content so it is important that we make it easy for the users to produce it. The full text of the message being replied to is shown so that selections may be included. The ability to include HTML-style tags allows a flexible approach to producing stylish messages. The 'preview' button allows the author to check how the message will look, while 'submit' commits the message to the board.

Building Community
In a face-to-face conversation there are many non-verbal cues to help decide whether to trust the other people involved in the exchange. When designing a text-only medium it is important to provide mechanisms that give these cues. On the Fool system we use stars after authors' names to indicate the number of messages they have posted, and provide a profile page (accessed by clicking on the user's name) where they may give information about themselves. Other people's views on this person are also useful, so the profile page shows the total

number of recommendations that this person's messages have received and the number of people who have them as a favourite. Possibly the most useful part of the profile is the feature that allows access to the last 99 messages written by this author.

Let us return for a moment to the message view page (Figure 3): next to the user's name are two buttons – a happy smiley face and a frowning one. To add the author of a message to my list of favourites I simply click the smiley face; to ignore messages by a particular person I click the frowning face.

We have already discussed how the reader may arrange the board view page by author or by recommendation. The Fool system also has special pages that aggregate this information across all boards. The 'view favourites' page allows the reader to follow the messages of their favourite authors across all boards. The 'best of the boards' page (Figure 5), on the other hand, allows readers to browse across boards having the most recommended messages displayed. They can do this for all boards, for those in a particular folder or for the boards in their list of favourites. The selection can be done across a time span of a day or a week, or between any arbitrary pair of dates.

Figure 5. The 'Best of Boards' page. Messages from many different boards are shown, giving the best messages of the day. It is also possible to select the best messages of the week, etc.

Administering the Discussion
The outcome of the recent court case Godfrey v. Demon 1999, in which Demon was sued because of defamatory material which had been posted on one of their newsgroups, has emphasised the requirement that those administering a community must be able to show that they respond promptly to any complaint of defamation, copyright infringement or other legal problems (Halberstam, 1999). To do otherwise is to become liable, as publisher, for the messages published by your members. It is tempting to consider running your discussion boards like a moderated news group, and reading each message before it is published. However, quite apart from the fact that this would be an enormous amount of work, and would make the discussion stilted, it might make the legal situation worse. The administrator of a discussion system could be liable, as the publisher, for what appears there. But by asserting editorial control a system administrator could be viewed as jointly accepting the author's liability, and hence be liable for defamation when messages appear, rather than when people complain. The recent adoption by Britain of the European Human Rights declaration may have an impact on free speech. So don't rely on me on this, I am a community producer, not a lawyer. Do get a proper legal opinion before embarking on administering a new discussion system. From a community management point of view the key to facilitating a healthy community is to provide leadership rather than control.

It is clear, though, that you need to provide a complaint mechanism. Ideally this should be automated and should keep an audit trail of who complains and how you respond. For a small community you could start with an informal e-mail-based mechanism. However, consider the situation where you receive a message which simply says: 'Someone on your boards has insulted my boss, Fred Smith, and we want the message removed.' Typically you will search your boards and find either no mention of Mr Smith or thousands of references to Fred Smiths of various sorts, leaving you unable to tell which is the Fred Smith in question and which messages are regarded as insulting. After dealing with a couple of complaints like this you will yearn for an automated system that links the complaint to a specific message.

On the Fool site we have a 'problem post' mechanism. A reader who objects to any message, or who thinks that a message transgresses our terms and conditions, may click the 'problem post' link to submit a private comment to the discussion board administrators. These comments are logged and sent on to our discussion board team who make a judgement as to how to respond. The options include:

- contacting the original author by e-mail and drawing his or her attention to our posting guidelines

- joining the public discussion on the board to guide it or comment on it
- in extreme cases, removing a message
- ultimately, cancelling the membership of a user who regularly has messages removed.

The other important role for the board administration on The Motley Fool is maintaining the links to the editorial material and the FAQ messages. The aim here is to link the informal discussion to the editorial content and ultimately to pre-emptively answer the questions that come up over and over again. The board administration principle is 'provide alternative sources for answers to the frequently asked questions in order to minimise the boredom amongst the regulars'.

Conclusion

A healthy community can help to create and retain a loyal reader base. These readers may become ambassadors for your site. I have talked about the principles of community, and about the planning, design and management of community-based web sites. In conclusion I will simply highlight the most important issues from each area.

- Planning – decide on the mission, identify the audience
- Design – aim to substitute for the cues provided in face-to-face conversation; provide tools for searching and navigating through a large collection of messages; help the user to make high quality contributions
- Management – aim for leadership rather than control of your community.

References

Alderman, J. 'MindVox on the Rocks' *Wired* 10 April 1997 (http://www.wired.com/news/topstories/0,1287,3085,00.html)

Cavanaugh, K. 'Mindvox, Long a Haven for Hackers, Signs Off' *CyberTimes* 13 July 1996 (http://www.evolution.com/press/cybertimes/)

Figallo, C. *Hosting Web Communities: Building Relationships, Increasing Customer Loyalty, and Maintaining A Competitive Edge*, New York, John Wiley & Sons, Inc., 1998

Hagel, J. and Armstrong, A. *Net Gain: Expanding Markets Through Virtual Communities*, Boston, Harvard Business School Press, 1997

Halberstam, S. 'Defamation and the Internet', 1999 (http://www.we-blaw.co.uk/art190499.htm) [Many other articles on this web site are also relevant]

Kim, A. J. *Community Building on the Web: Secret Strategies for Successful On-line Communities*, Berkeley, Peachpit Press, 2000

McDaid, E., O'Brien, W., Row, G. and Hashim, A. 'The TALENT Network Tutoring System', paper presented at *Telecommunications for Education and Training 1999*, Gjøvik, Norway, 8–11 June 1999

Rheingold, H. *The Virtual Community: Homesteading on the Electronic Frontier*, Boston, MIT Press, 1993 [Also at http://www.rheingold.com/vc/book/1.html]

OUT-LAW.COM

(http://www.out-law.com)

OUT-LAW.COM is a new media and e-commerce service that was set up by Masons, an international law firm with an IT law specialism, in May 2000. The web site provides free legal news, business guides and information, and invites businesses to contact the OUT-LAW team for an hour's free legal consultation.

The site was designed to offer information from the perspective of the target audience, i.e. people who want to know how the law affects their business without having to wade through legal jargon. Weekly e-mails are sent to registered users, updating them on the week's main legal and business news stories.

The site was set up principally by Iain Monaghan, Jon Fell and John Salmon, partners in Masons, Vincent Gray, Masons' marketing manager, and Struan Robertson, who joined the team as the site editor.

By Struan Robertson (Site Editor)

Frames: no	JavaScript: yes	Java: yes
Flash: no	Audio/video: no	Animation: yes
HTML editor: bespoke publishing system		
Database: MySQL		
FTP: n/a		Graphics: Photoshop
Server software: Linux OS, Apache Web Server		
Other software: Key Text macro generator		
Team: five-plus people		
History: launched May 2000		
Monthly page views: 12,500		
Site size: 500 pages approx		
Usability: optimised for all browsers		

Introduction

The site was set up to exploit what we saw as a gap in the market for legal information on line. Almost all the major UK law firms already had their own web sites, but most of these were on-line brochures for the firms themselves, providing little in the way of content. Where legal information was offered, it was often written in legal jargon and was difficult to find on the site without already knowing something about the topic. Our site was intended to focus on new media and e-commerce businesses and to present easy-to-read information according to the user's business type and business issues, not according to the legal topic. The plan was also to develop a brand that would appeal to businesses operating in the new economy.

Issues, Solutions and Outcomes

OUT-LAW the Service
OUT-LAW.COM is not just a web site; one of our objectives is to raise brand awareness for both OUT-LAW.COM and Masons and introduce new clients to the firm (because, basically, we are still a law firm). When deciding to set up our site we had to decide whether to do so as a company or partnership independent of Masons. Masons is a partnership bound by the rules of law societies. Ultimately, for practical and regulatory reasons, we decided to set up OUT-LAW.COM as a service within Masons: a separate brand within Masons, but not a separate legal entity. Clients of OUT-LAW.COM are also clients of Masons. OUT-LAW.COM has separate letterhead (although most correspondence is by e-mail) and the team members have both Masons and OUT-LAW.COM business cards.

The Brand
The firm was keen to create a separately branded service. The Masons brand was neither well known nor recognised by the market sector we were targeting with our new web site. In the minds of our target audience we were just another large law firm. We also recognised that a different approach to delivering legal services was required.

Finding a brand that appeals proved to be very important. The first thing we did was draw up our proposition and a brief summarising what we wanted to achieve from the brand. Ideas flowed from that. We were keen to create a true dotcom brand that would reflect the attitude of new media and e-commerce entrepreneurs. We eventually settled on OUT-LAW.COM, which encapsulated the entrepreneurial spirit of those involved with new media and e-commerce.

Once we had picked the brand, the next step was to do a simple domain name and trademark search. Our chosen domain name was already taken and in use, so we had the choice of either offering to buy it or choosing a different name. Fortunately, we were able to negotiate a reasonable price.

Although our brand is quite simple, a great deal of effort went into it. We took the views of clients and contacts before eventually settling on a logo in the shape of a sheriff's badge, which proved to be instantly identifiable and memorable. The brand identity was worked on by James Cameron of The Top Design Agency in Glasgow.

The OUT-LAW.COM logo.

Site Content

We were conscious that many information-based sites are launched with little information in the expectation that more will be added later. We wanted to make sure that we launched with as much content as possible, because if a site has little to offer a user on a first visit, that user is less likely to return. We were also conscious that many sites find they do not have the time to add as much content as they would like to after their launch. We spent many hours working out the best way to present our content. It was decided that it would be broken down into topics, each topic having one business guide that would provide an overview. Each guide would then have any number of articles that would go into more detail. We were fortunate in having a large number of people in Masons who could contribute content. Getting them to write it by the given deadline was, however, another matter. This was a problem with launching as a service within an established business – many staff saw the work for our site as something they could only justify doing in their spare time. The writing of content ultimately took much more effort and time than we had originally expected.

We were also conscious that too many sites are launched by off-line businesses and then quickly go 'stale'. We employed a full-time site editor to make sure this did not happen. It sounds obvious, perhaps, but very few of our competitor law firms do this.

We had many ideas for additional features on our site, but were conscious that we could not hope to do everything in the first phase. One thing we did offer from day one was a shoot-'em-up game, where players can zap lawyers, accountants and venture capitalists. The game has been a popular contrast to the more serious content on the site. It also helped distinguish our site from any competitor's site, which did no harm in attracting media coverage. Another media-friendly function of the site was to make our legal news available to WAP-enabled phones. The cost of offering the additional function was minimal compared with the benefit of it in terms of news coverage – and therefore free publicity – for our site.

Site Design

It took us a long time to think through how to present the information on our site. Clutter is dangerous on a web site, and perhaps more so on one that is information based.

The web interface design of OUT-LAW.COM was done by the Glasgow office of BlackID. They came up with the site's menu structure, graphics and overall presentation, having first given us a number of suggestions. With a name like OUT-LAW.COM it was important to get the right balance between a serious, corporate image on the one hand, and a less serious, informal image on the other. We felt that BlackID managed to get this the way we wanted it.

The back-end programming was done by Realise in Edinburgh. In the weeks before launch we were in almost constant communication with Realise's team. Our own team expected to work long hours as the launch date approached; that Realise were willing to do the same was a big reassurance.

Technology

OUT-LAW.COM is a dynamic, content-driven site. To provide for this Realise produced a unique site architecture that enabled us to have full editorial control over all aspects of content, layout and style. This was achieved by separating design completely from content. The content is stored within database tables and design is separated into templates with bespoke style tags.

The freedom and flexibility offered by this innovative publishing system give it an advantage over any of the traditional site-editing systems on the market. It reduces administration time and ensures that the design and content can be refreshed quickly.

The site needed to be fully searchable, so Realise used bespoke search engine technology based around knowledge portal software produced by Glowworm (http://www.glowworm.com). This software uses artificial intelligence, allowing users to search for data using natural language; it also delivers more relevant search results.

OUT-LAW.COM's WAP site uses the same content database tables to produce dynamic news content for WAP users.

When we launched the site we included a Flash intro. It was never intended to be permanent, but, like most Flash intros, it was a case of 'you've seen it once . . .', so we removed it after two weeks. Although we were targeting a sector that was more IT-savvy than most, we were surprised that so many people said they could not access the site because they didn't have Flash installed, despite the 'skip intro' or 'download Flash' options. It also proved irritating for those with slow Internet connections.

Another practical problem has been that of registration. We wanted people to register with us so we could gather information on who was using our site and then use that to develop the site and our marketing strategies in the firm. Finding a means to do that without scaring away the users proved more difficult than expected. Many people seemed to be sceptical that we would give away information for free and some did not initially register because they assumed there would be a charge. The wording of the invitation to register was soon changed to add the words 'for free'.

Updates to the site are straightforward: Struan, our site editor, can make changes to a preview site and at any time copy this site to the live site.

Time
One of the major development obstacles for us was finding the time to set up the site, since those initially involved still had their full-time 'normal' work to attend to. Struan came on board during the development phase, and at this stage was the only full-time resource on OUT-LAW.COM.

Preparing for Launch
We set a deadline for our site's launch and postponed it once (by approximately one month), then managed to stick to it. We were fairly satisfied with our project management along the way. Before the launch we were keen to ensure that everyone in Masons knew what we were doing, so we presented our plans to all the firm's offices. That proved very successful and everyone has been very supportive of the OUT-LAW.COM project.

Marketing and Promotion
There is no point in having a fantastic web site if no one looks at it. We decided on off-line, on-line and direct mail approaches. We devised a teaser campaign and placed adverts in the press. We also sent postcards to 4,000 targeted contacts and clients throughout the UK. On-line advertising involved sponsoring FT.com's Internet and e-commerce mailing list and also Silicon.com's Internet mailing list. This initial push was supported by an ongoing campaign to place stories about OUT-LAW.COM in the press.

We registered our site with search engines a number of weeks after launch. It was perhaps something we should have organised sooner, but we didn't attach a high priority to it, taking the view that our fairly narrow target audience was not likely to find us by chance. We took a number of quotes on registration, ranging from £100 to several thousand pounds. We quickly realised that registration is something of an art, and in the end decided to stick with Realise, who offered their own registration service.

Success

The site has already been a tremendous success, although the original idea was only conceived in Masons in November 1999, and the site was launched in May 2000. Frankly, we didn't know what reaction to expect.

To monitor traffic to the site, we use WebTrends software. We received 400,000 hits in our first month. 'Hits' is a slightly misleading term, as many people assume that it means the number of people who visit a site. What it really refers to is the traffic that a web server handles. A hit is a single file request in the access log of a web server, and this means that a request for one page can produce several hits if there are a lot of graphic images on that page. So one page impression can produce several hits. But we found that most of the press still likes to refer to 'hits' when gauging a site's success, so we provided our hit count. More realistic was the figure of 12,000 user sessions. The average time of a user session has varied over our first few months between 15 and 30 minutes; we are told that this is unusually high for a web site. It only took a few weeks for more than 2,000 people to register with the site. This might sound like a low figure, but we are under no illusions that OUT-LAW.COM will ever rival Amazon.com – ultimately, we are a legal information web site for new media and e-commerce businesses. There is a limit to the number of people that want that sort of information.

Before the launch we did not plan for the dissemination of our content to other sites, and the number of other web sites and off-line publications that want to use our guides and our daily news content has surprised us. OUT-LAW's news is now circulated to several journalists on a daily basis.

The site invites feedback, which has been excellent (the same has been true of press reports on the site). At worst, our feedback included the odd comment like 'interesting site'. Some more constructive criticism might be helpful!

Most importantly for us, the site has introduced new business to the firm. Since the launch we have rolled out our service to support our Hong Kong office. This involved providing the business guides based on a choice of UK or Hong Kong law in such a way that the ease of use of the site was not compromised. In both the UK and Hong Kong we have seen many new clients approach us for work.

We are presently working on the second phase of our site, the main development of which will involve selling contracts on-line. Putting the payment mechanisms in place for what we intend to do will add a new dimension to our site.

'Get ahead and stay ahead in the new economy' is our site motto: we have achieved part one – the challenge is to stay there.

The National Gallery

(http://www.nationalgallery.org.uk)

The National Gallery houses the national collection of Western European paintings. It has around 2,300 pictures and covers every European school of painting from about 1260 through to 1900. The new web site, designed by Lateral, aims to be deceptively simple; to quote the Lateral web site, the intention was to create 'a masterwork of clarity, with effortless navigation and an abundance of rich detail'.

By Simon Crab and David Hart (Web Designers, Lateral)

Frames: yes	JavaScript: yes	Java: no
Flash: no	Audio/video: no	Animation: yes
HTML editor: Adobe GoLive, BBEdit		
Design: Lateral		
Usability: optimised for all browsers		

The original design brief from the National Gallery was twofold:

- Represent the National Gallery collection on the Internet in the best possible light
- Educate people who come to the gallery so that they can view the collection more efficiently (rather than encouraging more people to come to the gallery, as there are enough visitors already).

The design was to be for a completely new site, as the first part of a three-phase development strategy.

The clients specified that download speed and image quality were of the highest importance. Satisfying these two potentially conflicting requirements implies a compromise, because large files do not load as quickly as small files, but small files cannot carry the same level of visual information. To ensure the best outcome all the images were 'hand compressed', rather than being batch processed, to allow for the best image quality versus download speed for each individual image. It was also decided to make all paintings viewable at three different sizes: thumbnail (typically 60 pixels square), medium (200 pixels) and full size (400 pixels). This permitted viewers to first get a general idea of the type of painting in each collection, and then choose to click and zoom in on the higher quality images.

Screenshots from the National Gallery web site showing how the three sizes of image provide different views of each work: the thumbnails are used in the context of the collection; the mid-sized images appear within a descriptive page; and the largest images provide a full-screen view for closer inspection.

The design specification required that the site be suitable for users with 44 kbps modem connections, meaning that our target page size was approximately 40–50 kb (in total), enabling pages to load in about a second. We assumed that the target audience would not be particularly web literate and would be using domestic equipment (e.g. Pentium I, 90 MHz, 800×600 screen resolution on a 16-bit monitor).

The site navigation had to be clear and easy to use to accommodate this target group, with nothing on the site being too clever or gimmicky – the aim was for straightforward, minimum-click navigation. The design of the 'non painting' parts of the site in particular was kept clear and uncluttered with flat colours for fast download times. This allowed the sections and pages with paintings to stand out by comparison – it was always important that the paintings were not overshadowed by the design/navigation used on the site. We also avoided the somewhat predictable and obvious 'virtual tour' of the gallery. Another design decision was based on the view that physical location of a painting (e.g. which room it was in) was irrelevant when viewing the web site, and so we grouped the paintings into collections.

As a design agency Lateral has general site performance criteria in terms of technology and design. These criteria are adapted for different clients according to their specific requirements, but in general they serve as the basic guideline for everything we do.

Effective site performance is quite easy to achieve with this in mind, as it is mostly common sense, with the designer aiming for usability by the lowest common denominator of technology: trying out the site with a modem on a low-specification PC for example. We do pride ourselves on building workable sites, rather than technical showcases, and so we work hard to avoid huge irrelevant graphics and frivolous plug-ins. The general aim at all times is to meet the clients' objectives.

There are always some restrictions that limit the entirely free hand a designer might prefer. For example, there was a history of design/presentation for the National Gallery that was followed: the 'art' from our point of view came in not breaking or seeking to reinvent the National Gallery brand but in manipulating it for a new medium – the Internet.

The whole site was built using 'traditional' tools: Adobe GoLive (version 2 at the time) was used to for production speed (we built the site in two weeks) and the code was cleaned up using BBEdit. The JavaScript was also written with BBEdit. No database technology was used because the second phase of the site is to be a larger database-driven project.

Initially we updated the site by hand, and later taught National Gallery staff how to maintain and update the site in house.

Other than maintaining the National Gallery brand, there were few design limitations imposed by either the client or the nature of the content – if design gets in the way of the content then something has gone wrong in the design process. It would have been useful to be able to add a content management system from the start of this project, but budgetary constraints mean that this will have to wait until later.

As designers we try to work very closely with clients at the initial stages of a project, so that we can agree on an initial specification and working practices. This process is based on the 'default' project process document that we have built up over the years. The National Gallery project worked out efficiently, due not least to the fact that there were National Gallery staff who were both knowledgeable and enthusiastic about the web site and its development.

Since the site management and updating has been taken in-house, new elements and features have been added that we would not have necessarily chosen, and this is often the case if an outsourced project then gets managed by the client themselves. The benefit of taking on the management of the site is of course the ability to make changes quickly and easily and add parts of the site as necessary, or as user needs or collections and services develop.

The key issue for a site manager when dealing with design agencies is trust: once the project specification has been agreed the manager must feel safe in letting the designers get on with it, in the knowledge that they are experts in their field.

Web Site Policies and E-Commerce

Sites that collect payment, registration or other customer information have an absolute need to ensure that the site is secure and that data is dealt with appropriately. Stated policies which confirm to the user that the site is aware of the risks – and user concerns – need to be clear and unambiguous.

Policies

A September 2000 report from Gigaweb (http://www.gigaweb.com) showed that 66 per cent of web sites failed to provide a link to a privacy policy. If your site receives payments, collects personal details or requires users to register, you should make a very explicit statement on your policies. Ensure that every question asked is asked for a purpose. Do you really need to know the age or salary of site visitors? Does it matter how often they use the Web? Asking too many intrusive questions may lead to respondents just selecting anything to get through the form, thus undermining the accuracy of the data.

You should establish and publish policies on the following:

- Data protection and privacy
- Security
- Continuity
- Copyright.

They do not need to be particularly complicated or extensive documents, but they should address three elements – legal obligations, technical details and user expectations.

Most commercial sites now have their policies placed prominently on their site: many use a standard form of wording that could be used as the basis for your own policy (without simply copying of course).

Data Protection and Privacy Policy

- What information is gathered about your visitors?
- What do you do with the information gathered?
- With whom do you share the information, if anyone?

- What is your opt-out policy?
- What is your policy on correcting and updating personally identifiable information?
- What is your policy on deleting or deactivating names from the database?

The USA has the Children's Online Protection Act, which requires web sites to get parental consent before collecting information from children aged 12 or younger. This is perhaps only relevant if your site is specifically US-focused, but the principles are sound.

TRUSTe (http://www.truste.org) provides an on-line wizard to enable you to construct a very detailed statement on privacy and information collection. They offer a certification service – for a fee. The site also includes information on all aspects of privacy.

Security Policy

Secure server explain how and why payments are secured

- Credit card transactions – explain the guarantee from the credit card company, and possibly extend it with your own, as Amazon does, to underwrite the first £50.00 as well
- Encryption – describe which level of encryption your site has, in simple terms: you are trying to impress and reassure the user, not give secrets away to potential hackers
- Alternative methods of payment – these can maximise revenue but add to the administrative burden. You will need to assess the costs and benefits of offering a range of payment methods
- Refund policy – make it clear how this operates.

As with privacy, site visitors will have a natural concern with the security of your on-line payment system. It can seem risky to give credit card details to a stranger, especially one whose web site may be in a different country.

You also need to protect yourself from fraudulent customers: Protx (http://www.protx.com) and Cybersource (http://www.cybersource.com) both offer some defence against fraudulent transactions through verified payment systems and databases of fraudsters.

Continuity Policy

- Updates policy – if the content on the site is perishable, then there should be an easy method for the visitor to notify the site manager that an error has occurred, that facts have changed, that something is simply wrong

- Contact details for web site manager – it is good relationship marketing to positively encourage feedback and contributions from the audience. They feel that you listen to their needs and suggestions; you get the benefit of thousands of proof-readers! A truly confident web site manager would offer a small reward for notification of errors.

Copyright Policy

- Copyright statement – a simple statement of ownership
- Protection and limitations – specifying the restrictions, permissions and licences available for use of content from the site (if any)
- Images – some sites may also licence use of images for personal or charity use.

All web design staff need to be trained in and kept up-to-date with copyright issues. Protecting your own copyright is one thing – infringement of others' copyright may result in expensive, embarrassing and damaging publicity.

- Rights to be respected include those of authorship, integrity and privacy
- Credit should always be given and work should only used when it is meant for public broadcast, and then in a non-derogatory way
- Downloading and then editing or re-using images, sound, video and text from the Web may be technically possible but is not usually legal, unless specific permission is obtained from the page owner or images are explicitly 'public domain'
- Trademarks belonging to other companies must not be used without their authorisation.

The Copyright Licensing Agency (http://www.cla.co.uk) provides useful background information on all aspects of copyright and licensing, including the implications of electronic publishing.

Disclaimers

- The web site might have a disclaimer on its own content, affirming that information is there for consideration at the user's risk, and that it might be out of date, or should be checked with an appropriate professional adviser. This might be linked from every page, or just on the home page
- External links should carry a simple reminder that they are outside the control of the site, and therefore should be treated with caution
- E-mails should also carry a brief disclaimer, which might include statements that the opinions do not necessarily reflect official

organisational policy, or that the writer does not have the authority to enter in to contractual agreements on the organisation's behalf.

The Standard for E-Commerce

Two hundred global merchants, led by Ziff-Davis, have combined to create a standard for Internet commerce, with the overriding aim of establishing and promoting customer satisfaction, confidence and trust. Although the formal standard itself (http://www.gii.com/standard/index.html) may not be entirely appropriate for all web sites, the key principles should be adopted as good practice. Many of the recommendations and requirements of the standard correspond to the requirements of the Which? Web Trader Scheme (http://www.which.com/webtrader/), which seeks to encourage traders to adopt an effective code of practice that supports and protects on-line consumers.

For example, sites should have an easily identified information centre, where visitors can find the merchant name, legal identity and ownership, physical location and contact details, as well as relevant professional licences.

A set of information should be provided, much of which has already been discussed in this chapter, but which includes:

- Information on all charges, including tax, shipping and insurance
- Information on warranties or guarantees
- Information on available product and service support
- Applicable law and jurisdiction for the merchant
- Payment options
- Cancellation, return and refund policies
- Credit card charging policy
- Policies on privacy, personal data and security
- Details of ordering and fulfilment process, including charges and notification of shipping and/or delays
- Customer service policy and complaints procedure
- Access by customer to account and order status.

Many of these require technical solutions, but most are management issues that should be addressed by most web sites, whether or not they are conducting transactions and selling products or services.

Marketing and Promotion

Web site promotion is not a single event, but a continuous process. As with 'real world' marketing activities, it is part of the ongoing life of the organisation. No single activity guarantees success, rather it is the combination of promotional techniques that builds site traffic over time

---

Maximising Web Site Traffic

Your audience will determine which promotional strategy is most effective, but there is a group of actions that can be applied to almost all web sites, whether or not they have a substantial marketing budget. Even if your service is not actively competing with similar sites, you are still competing with the rest of the Web for your audience's time and attention. Being easily found is as much about customer service as it is about competitiveness – the more easily you can be found, the better the service to those who know about you, the better the impression on those who do not.

> 'The Internet is like a big city full of blindfolded people. No one will know your site is there unless you tell them.'
>
> **Liz Citron**
> **MD, Arehaus**

There are ten key ways to attract attention to your web site: some will be more effective than others, and some are definitely more time-consuming or expensive than others. All should at least be considered, and then implemented – as far as possible, practical or affordable.

Off-line promotion

    Release

    Include

    Advertise

On-line promotion

    Link

    Design

    Submit

Promotion by communication

>   E-mail and newsletters

>   Discussion lists

>   Communities

And finally ...

>   Promotion by design

Off-Line Promotion

These three activities are ones that any organisation might undertake, regardless of whether it has a web site.

Release

- Press releases to all stakeholders – customers, suppliers, staff, owners – as well as the media
- Launch events – a new web site, or a new development within a web site, might be an opportunity for an event, or for a formal launch at a conference or exhibition
- Competitions – off-line competitions involving the web site, perhaps some form of short quiz based on web content, designed to force participants to at least explore the site
- Trade and professional media – always looking for relevant industry news, so more likely to feature your site than national media outlets
- Internet media and supplements – if your site has an unusual example of some feature, or is particularly novel, then contact the general Internet magazines for a brief mention – or even a case study.

The leading Internet magazines – *Internet Works, Internet Magazine, .Net* – and the others all list dozens of new sites in each issue. Several are also included in the broadsheet weekly Internet supplements.

Internet Resources Newsletter (http://www.hw.ac.uk/libWWW/irn/irn.html) lists several dozen new sites each month, and reaches several thousand readers – and it's free. It's less appropriate for pure commercial sites perhaps, but suitable for those that have relevance to the academic and research community

Include

- E-mail signature – sending out an e-mail without an effective signature file is like writing a business letter on plain paper. The signature should contain a link to the web site as well as other contact details. Ensure that all staff in the organisation have an effective signature

- All stationery items both for internal and external use should carry the URL
- Vehicles, shop-front and print advertising should incorporate the URL
- Switchboard operators should be informed of the web site and its contents, as indeed should all staff
- Giveaways, souvenirs and other exhibition or course materials.

Everyone who deals with your organisation should be aware that there is information available on your web site. They should have a general idea of what is available, and of course they need to know how to access it.

Advertise

- Posters – depending on the web site, advertising on the tube, on buses or on billboards may be appropriate (budget permitting)
- Printed newsletters, inserts and flyers – more affordable than media advertising in many cases, and also better targeted
- Banner adverts – individually negotiated banner adverts on specific web sites can be useful, although more general banner advertising has a very low click-through rate and may therefore only be of limited effectiveness. Careful consideration as to cost and effectiveness is needed, but if a relevant site can be identified it can bring interested and informed visitors your way (as opposed to general sightseers). Costs range from £15 to £60 CPM (per thousand impressions)
- Radio advertising can be surprisingly affordable, particularly for short concentrated campaigns, with a 30-second slot costing as little as £30 on local stations.

If you are EasyJet, you can start a chain of cyber-cafés to promote your airline. If you are the BBC, you can get every programme to mention your URL. If you are Dixons, you can give away CDs from every shop. All of these are good examples of cross-promotion.

On-Line Promotion

While the three off-line activities have budgetary implications, the three key on-line activities are essentially free, costing only staff time to implement.

Link

Links operate in two directions, both of which can be harnessed to promote your site.

Out-Bound Links

A useful page of out-bound links – as well as context-related links within the content – can greatly enhance the site. There are only four ways in which to leave a site: click on the 'Back' button, click on the 'Home' button, enter a new URL in the location box, or follow a link provided by the site. (Of course, you could also close the browser window or turn off the PC.) Following a link is the only one of these that is a positive action, reinforcing the usefulness of your site. Create a categorised and annotated set of links, and you are adding a useful area of content to the site, one that gives visitors a reason to return. They are then using your site as a launch-pad for a web session, and have another reason to tell friends and colleagues about you.

In-Bound Links

Links from other sites in to your site are becoming increasingly important, because more and more search engines use the number of in-bound links as one of their ranking measures – the more links you have, the higher your site is placed in search results, on the grounds that the more sites that link to you, the better you must be.

You can exploit this trend by encouraging in-bound links – ask visitors to link to you, and make it easier by providing a page which shows the code required to create a link. This is how many of the search engines generate a presence on other sites.

You should also follow a deliberate programme of contacting other web sites, through their web master's e-mail address, and inviting them to link to you, perhaps offering a link in return. To identify suitable sites use a link-counting service, such as LinkCount (http://www.linkcount.com) or LinkPopularity (http://www.linkpopularity.com), which checks the search engines for links to a particular site. Use these services to see who already links to you – and check that they are not saying anything inappropriate about you. But more usefully, identify sites you could regard as competition for visitors, use these services to see who links to them, then e-mail those sites requesting a link to your site as well.

> 'Measure your success it's always useful to analyse how many sites link to you. LinkPopularity (http://www.linkpopularity.com) lets you check on the number of sites that have hyperlinks to you.'
>
> **Marieke Napier**
> Information Officer, UKOLN and Editor, *Exploit Interactive* and *Cultivate Interactive* web magazines

LinkCount compares two sites, whilst LinkPopularity compares results for a single site from three search engines.

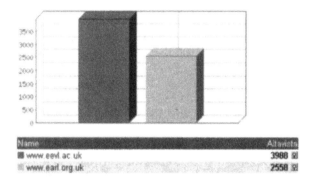

Name	AltaVista
■ www.eevl.ac.uk	3980 🔍
▨ www.earl.org.uk	2558 🔍

Source: LinkCount (http://www.linkcount.com)

This example shows a comparison between EEVL and EARL, and clicking on the magnifying glass icon would take you to AltaVista to see the link details.

You should also check your site statistics to see where your visitors come from, then see if those sites will put a more prominent link in place.

Specific banner advert swaps with related sites are simply graphical reciprocal links. Visitors from 'hard' links are likely to be actively interested – they have after all clicked on a link to get to you – so they may be higher value visitors than those who come from search engine results. Focus your energy accordingly.

Design

A lot of energy is expended on getting to a high position in the search engine results rankings. This can be very productive if your site is in a specialist area, or has certain unique topics, but can be difficult to do successfully in more competitive sectors. Nevertheless, you should certainly go through the process of designing-in searchability to give your site the best possible chance of being visible in the results.

The search engines organise their rankings according to the relationship between the search terms – the keywords – and the content of the pages in their index. Optimising your pages for the search engines involves two distinct steps: identifying the appropriate keywords, and placing them appropriately in the page.

Identifying Keywords

Keywords are the terms used by searchers for which you would like to be the result. This does not necessarily match with how you would describe your site yourself. A recruitment company, for example, might describe itself as 'executive search' but if the users search for 'head hunter' then that is the keyword they need to use to achieve a match, no matter how little they may like the term.

The search engine GoTo (http://www.goto.com) has a useful keyword suggestion tool that helps identify appropriate search terms: search for three or four alternatives and see how often those terms were used in the last month. The tool also suggests related keywords that might be effective in focusing your keyword placement. The search illustrated here included searches for 'head hunter', 'executive search' and 'executive jobs'. It shows that 'head hunter' is searched for ten times more often.

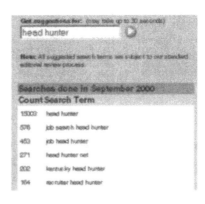

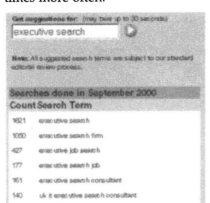

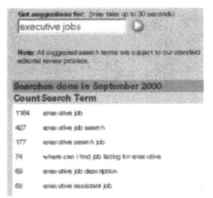

Source: GoTo (http://www.goto.com)

GoTo is one of the top-ten search engines by usage, and so its results may be taken as a reasonable approximation of how search terms are used.

Placing Keywords
Once you have identified a group of keywords, the next stage is to place them on your web pages.

- **<meta> tags**
  <meta name="description" content = "A concise and meaningful description of the site, that is presented as a search result.">
  <meta name = "keywords" content = "relevant, meaningful, numerous, words and phrases, essential, considered, well chosen">

'<alt> tags are extremely important for search engines. Any images on your pages should have a stack of information in the <alt> tags about what your site does. This will boost your position in the search engines.'

Matt Martell
ContentGenerators

Many search engines do not give <meta> tags any great prominence as they can be used misleadingly, but they are still indexed as part of the body text. The description is important because it is used as the text in the search results.

- **URL, <title>, headings**
  Placing keywords in the <title>, URL (if possible) and in <h1> heading tags will give the keyword a higher score

- **Image alt tags**
  As well as enabling accessibility, placing the keywords sensibly in the alt attribute gives a few more opportunities for the search engine to see them.

- **Doorway or bridge pages**
  These are pages specifically designed to meet the needs of the search engines, and so are loaded (but not stuffed) with appropriate keywords. Each page, however, simply links to the existing home or menu page, providing a one-way guide into the site. You can create several of these, each focused on a different aspect of your services and therefore covering different groups of keywords.

Some points to watch:

- Avoid over-repetition of keywords as some search engines will penalise you

- Not all search engines use keywords – Excite specifically does not, for example

- Use variants – different capitalisation, alternative spelling, even typos

- Avoid using clever tricks, such as repeating keywords, or hiding keywords in background colours, in tiny text or as the alt tag to invisible gifs. The search engines are aware of these tricks and will penalise pages that use them.

Because some search engines no longer regard <meta> tags as meaningful, a lot of effort can be wasted trying to force pages up the search results. It is useful to check which features are supported by the different search engines, and most give some guidance as to how to design pages for effective retrieval. The best single source for this information is Search Engine Watch (http://www.searchenginewatch.com), which provides useful features such as comparison tables that specify how the different search engines index and rank their searches.

Submit

The search services mentioned below probably account for over 80 percent of searches, so ensure you are indexed by them. Also register your site with the leading UK-based services, and any industry specific directories relevant to your area of activity. And don't forget listings by hobbyists, company and trade sites and trade associations and other organisations. They all need their listing to be better than the others, so most invite submissions.

Indexes

AltaVista (http://www.altavista.com)	Northern Light (http://www.nlsearch.com)	Go (http://ww.go.com)
Google (http://www.google.com)	GoTo (http://www.goto.com)	Excite (http://www.excite.com)
Fast (http://www.alltheweb.com)	Lycos (http://www.lycos.com)	Webcrawler (http://www.webcrawler.com)
AOL (http://search.aol.com)	MSN (http://search.msn.com)	HotBot (http://www.hotbot.com)

Some of these share a base index and some share ownership, but they operate largely independently of each other. Search Engine Watch also provides listings showing which are the most popular, on a month-by-month basis.

GoTo (http://www.goto.com) differs from the other search indexes because it lets you bid to be listed at the top of the search results. For as little as $25 you can bid from $0.01 per result, which you only pay if the searcher follows the link. This cost is for specific keywords or phrases, so you can overcome the difficulties of highly competitive sectors if you feel it appropriate. For example, it would cost you 57¢ to top the list for a search for 'estate agent', $2.40 for 'insurance' and just 11¢ for 'actuaries'.

Directories

Yahoo (http://www.yahoo.com)	LookSmart (http://www.looksmart.com)	About (http://www.about.com)
Open Directory (http://dmoz.org)	WWW Virtual Library (http://vlib.org)	Infogrid (http://www.infogrid.com)

The directories act very differently to the search indexes – they are compiled by individuals, who apply listing criteria and some quality threshold. On a directory site, go to the subject page where you think your site should be listed, and follow the 'suggest a site' link from there. LookSmart requires a payment of $200 for submission at present; Yahoo requires a similar payment for express consideration, but will list you for no cost if you are prepared to wait – and if your site meets their criteria. Because of the importance of these two directories, a combined cost of $400 may actually be well worth the payment.

UK-Based Services

Search UK (http://www.searchuk.com)	UK Plus (http://www.ukplus.co.uk)	UK Max (http://www.ukmax.co.uk)
UK Index (http://www.ukindex.co.uk)	UK Directory (http://www.ukdirectory.co.uk)	AltaVistaUK (http://uk.altavista.com)
G.O.D. (http://www.god.co.uk)	YahooUK (http://www.yahoo.co.uk)	

If your organisation is UK-based it is sensible to submit to the leading UK-specific search services, as the sheer volume of competition will be reduced.

Submission Services
Paid-for submission services can quickly add you to hundreds of search services, but these will mostly be very obscure. However, once submission to the main services is completed it may be worth aiming for a truly comprehensive submissions policy, depending on budget and time. Best practice is normally to submit your site manually to the sites listed here, and then to evaluate your results after a few weeks as your pages start to feature in the search results.

To ensure that all your content pages are indexed by the search engines create a listings page, or submit your site index page.

Promotion by Communication

E-Mail and Newsletters

E-Mail
E-mail marketing is a very effective method of communicating with your audience. Even if you are not pushing a product for sale, regular contact with your users keeps your site uppermost in their thoughts and gives you an opportunity to show off your latest developments. As long as the mailing list is opt-in, i.e. voluntary, and the messages themselves are concise, relevant and useful, then your recipients will be happy to get the message – even if they don't need that particular snippet of information at that particular time. This all contributes to their feeling part of your community.

Newsletters

An e-mail newsletter is essentially a discussion list that is set to receive messages only from the list-owner. As a regular communication containing useful information to a subscriber list who have opted-in to receive it, it can be a powerful community-building tool.

Simple design guidelines can ensure that a newsletter performs as effectively as a fully formatted web page or print edition.

- Use a 'hook', such as a special offer or key article or topic, to attract the busy reader who may be scanning through a large set of e-mails
- Stick to a single topic to allow some focus
- Use a short and succinct writing style
- Use plain text, as not all e-mail users can cope with HTML-formatted e-mails
- Improve the look of the e-mail with simple formatting using spacing and keyboard characters (tabs, dotted lines etc)
- Start with important elements – time is too short to read a vague non-specific e-mail looking for a relevant feature
- Short (non-wrapping) URLs and short lines will ensure the best and most consistent appearance in all e-mail clients
- Offer an unsubscribe route in every issue, as well as contact details.

> 'Save yourself a lot of aggravation (especially if you run an automated mailing list) by pre-validating e-mail addresses. An excellent free Perl script for this is at http://www.TessPub.com/scripts.'
>
> **Elliot Manley**
> **MoltenGold**

FreePint (http://www.freepint.co.uk) is an example of a highly successful newsletter that breaks many of the guidelines above, but has built a large and loyal subscriber base (30,000+). The main guideline it breaks is that of length, typically printing out at 12–13 pages. FreePint is in many ways less an e-mail newsletter, more of a professional journal that just happens to be delivered by e-mail.

> 'Don't underestimate the power of e-mail communication. Regardless of whether it's a regular newsletter, an update or simply speedy responses to customer queries, all communication should be respectful and of the highest quality. If your e-mails contain useful information then users may even pass them on viral marketing is very powerful, after all.'
>
> **William Hann**
> **Managing Editor, Free Pint**

A discussion forum and extensive archives, book reviews and other resources on the supporting web site all demonstrate how the newsletter and the web site are mutually beneficial and dependent. The contributions by practitioners – articles, reviews, discussions – help establish it as a community publication. FreePint is an excellent example of viral marketing, spreading by word of mouth as well as through advertising. It also demonstrates 'magnetic marketing' – just as a piece of metal becomes magnetised by proximity to a magnet, and thence magnetises other metal items, so the community aspect of FreePint starts a virtuous circle: the more readers and contributors FreePint has, the more useful it is to the community, and so the more readers it attracts.

Discussion Lists

E-mail discussion lists provide a more private community discussion arena than newsgroups or message boards, as the postings arrive in individual subscriber's e-mail in-boxes, allowing them to respond as necessary and at their own convenience. Services such as eGroups (http://www.egroups.com) and JiscMail (http://www.jiscmail.ac.uk) host hundreds of discussion lists, along with their archives and membership lists. These can be kept private or made available to all interested parties.

The web site manager can use discussion lists in two ways:

- **Create and host a list**
  By hosting a discussion the site manager establishes credibility and acts as a mentor to a particular interest sectors. Light moderation to keep the list on topic and prevent it degenerating into arguments is essential in the best-run lists. The archive and list information provide useful content for the web site, and the list address can be a useful constant reminder of the parent web site.

- **Participate in existing lists**
  Careful and appropriate participation in existing lists can provide an opportunity to promote your site, as long as the promotion is delivered discreetly. Some participants do not mention their site at all, and leave it to their e-mail signature to lead the curious to their site; others are a little more explicit, which is fine as long as their site is relevant to the current discussion.

Communities

Members of web communities are more than just customers, suppliers, staff and stakeholders: they are active participants in the development of the site itself. As The Motley Fool case study demonstrates, the community develops from a site with a coherent look and feel, with a focus for the community to gather around. Whichever technology is involved – chat, message board or discussion list – it is the human intervention that develops mere messages in to a com-

'A lot of ISPs will claim only to allow scripted CGI programs, rather than compiled binaries. Now if you want to run anything fancy in Perl, then good luck and may your users be patient … But if you can, persuade their tech support department to let you install Ceilidh (http://www.lilikoi.com) it's a discussion forum that does exactly what it claims (to offer free threaded bulletin boards with file attachment and e-mail), and it saved me weeks of hassle. One of its best features is that it support the uploading of attachments to postings, a great way of getting content on to a site without having to encode it!'

Oliver Bond
DotGain

munity. The technology might be simple CGI scripts or a service hosted by a company such as Everyone.net (http://www.everyone.net) that lets users establish discussion forums, message boards and chat rooms.

A sense of continuity and belonging, careful seeding of discussion topics and delicate moderation by the hosting company are all essential to the development of a happy community.

Key conditions and features help the community develop:

- A compelling reason to join and stay
- Regular new topics
- Hands-off moderation, guiding rather than managing, but offering expertise when necessary
- FAQs and archives providing access to the shared history of the group
- Institutional participants who are not too sensitive to criticism
- Patience and encouragement
- Easy access and easy exit
- An accessible style – Motley Fool's particular specialty!

The benefits of marketing by communication are clear – you can build a more loyal community which feels a sense of ownership and collaboration with the web site's owners, and which is therefore ideally placed for future marketing activities.

And Finally ...

Promotion by Design

One grossly overlooked method of promotion is simply that of providing a good experience. A clear, easily navigated web site that does what it promises and makes it easy for visitors to accomplish their goals is worth hundreds of clever promotional techniques.

- Make it clear
- Make it work
- Make it worth returning.

Monitoring Search Engine Placings

As with any activity, you should monitor its effectiveness to see if your activities have been successful. Simply trying to search for your own site can be a frustrating process, as you will need to look through enormous numbers of results to see where your site is listed. Fortunately there are some tools to make this task easier.

> 'Search engines can point users to pages deep inside your site Always design your site allow users to be able navigate the site from any possible entry page.'
>
> **Eddie Stewart**
> **Web Master, DERA**

Did-it Detective (http://www.did-it.com/detective.htm) is an e-mail-based results service which lets you submit your details, then e-mails you your placings on the top dozen search services, as shown below:

Sample search placings on Did-It Detective			
AltaVista	1	AOLNetFind	>100
Excite	>100	GoTo	>100
HotBot	20	Infoseek	>100
Lycos	1	MSN	1
Snap	1	WebCrawler	>100
Yahoo	1		

Source: Did-it Detective (http://www.did-it.com/detective.htm)

Another service that provides you with instant results in a graphical format is PositionAgent (http://www.positionagent.com), which takes your keywords and matches them against your web site URL on eight of the top search engines. As with so many Web services, you can also apply this to your competitors to assess their effectiveness for specific keywords.

Results from PositionAgent

Monitoring Web Site Performance

Every web server keeps detailed site statistics in its log files. These give the starting point for assessing the effectiveness both of the web site and of your marketing activities. As well as measuring the simple performance statistics, you need to assess them in terms of your site's stickiness.

Sticky Web Sites

There are three basic measures of stickiness for a web site:

- **Time on the site**
  Content-heavy web sites should encourage visitors to stay longer than on other sites, in order to find and read the content. If the site is mostly composed of external links, then the time spent on the site may be greatly reduced.

- **Page views**
  The number of pages seen by a visitor also provides a measure of a site's stickiness: exploring the site for more and more information, the user is happy to spend some time reading a number of different pages – or possibly looking at a large number of products or services.

- **Repeat visits**
  This is a true measure of value for a site – if visitors return repeatedly, then your site must be offering an experience worth repeating.

Sites that are more commercial hope to translate the length of the visit into sales, but information-based sites will be content to establish a continuing relationship with the visitor. Designing a site to maximise stickiness involves providing useful content that is changed and updated frequently, so that it is worth reading and worth returning for the next set of information.

You need to determine the following information from your site statistics:

- Hits for each page
- How many individual users visit the site
- Average time that each page is looked at
- Do site changes increase or decrease traffic?
- Which advertising works (from source of traffic)?
- Busiest times, and days of week
- Paths through the site taken by a visitor

'Consider all the factors when analysing statistics. People may be not going to a section because the name you gave it was misleading, not because they aren't interested in that information.'

Liz Citron
MD, Arehaus

- Users' Internet addresses to determine their country and domain of origin (commercial, academic or non-profit for example)
- Errors delivered to visitors.

This information is needed to ascertain:

- The effectiveness of your design, your content and your marketing activities
- Whether you need to focus more on a particular part of your site
- Whether an expected type or part of your audience is missing
- Whether part of your content is simply unread.

The raw data should be available as log files on your web server. Some service providers may provide an interpreted version of this data, others leave it to you to analyse the data using WebTrends or a similar analysis package.

At a much simpler level, you could attach a counter graphic to a page – this might display the number of page views and give some extra information on your visitors, although you will only get a proportion of the full data. Visible counters such as those from HitBox (http://www.hitbox.com), theCounter.com (http://www.thecounter.com) or FXWeb (http://www.fxweb.com) have a tendency to look a little amateurish, as though you are trying to impress with big numbers. However with the more discreet versions, such as NedStat (http://www.nedstat.com) or IpStat (http://www.ipstat.com), a small logo provides links to useful information about site traffic, visitor location (at country level), and technical information about browsers and operating systems that might inform some aspects of page design. Most free counters offer a password-protected private version for a small fee.

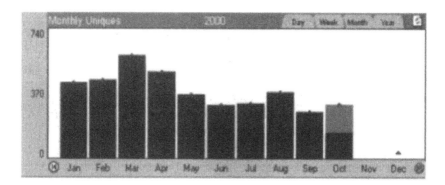

HitBox statistics for http://www.sable.co.uk/taxi/

Statistics cannot always be taken at face value, and will need some interpretation. For example, the results below contradict the browser statistics described in the early part of this book – in fact this is because the majority of users of this site are from the academic sector, where Netscape is still heavily used.

Return Visitor Percentages (determined by Persistent Cookies)			
One Time	82%	4-7 Times	1%
2-3 Times	9%	8+ Times	8%

Browser Percentages	
Netscape	52%
MSIE	47%
Mosaic	0%
Amiga-Based	0%
Other	0%
Unknown	1%

Operating System Predominance	
Windows 95, 98, NT, 2K	92%
Windows 3.1	4%
Macintosh	3%
Amiga	0%
Unix (X11)	0%
Non-Computer	0%

FXWeb statistics for http://www.sbu.ac.uk/training/

Monitor, evaluate, improve – this is a standard triangle of the marketing process. Every activity should be measured and assessed as far as possible, with the results being used to inform decisions on future activities.

Conclusion

The development of most web sites is a strange journey – there is usually a fairly definite starting point, and there are certainly planned destinations, unplanned diversions, unexpected delays and occasional disasters. But only unsuccessful sites reach journey's end – the best sites develop and evolve continuously, both in content and style, as the needs and expectations of the users grow and mature.

What I hope this book illustrates is that there are few perfect answer to many web site management issues. The range of solutions can seem as wide as the range of sites seeking them, but by seeing how others achieve their targets you can develop effective web sites that meet your objectives. Simply copying content, ideas and features can be seen with some justification as plagiaristic. But failing to learn and benefit from other's experiences is to rob yourself of one of the most rewarding elements of the Internet – the ability to share and develop with the assistance of a community of like-minded professionals. Those who generously contributed the case studies and submitted the tips and tricks included in this book provide ample evidence of this community's generosity.

Appendix

E-Mail Newsletters and Web-Based Advice

If you can bear the thought of yet more e-mail, there are many newsletters and discussion lists which bring expert advice and support direct to your in-box. Check out the supporting web site first: the best and most useful newsletters are those with searchable archives, and with careful use of those archives you could just avoid the in-box clutter. For those who regularly forget to check the most useful sites, a weekly reminder that nudges you gently may be just what is needed.

Mailbase Discussion Lists (http://www.mailbase.ac.uk)
There are many useful lists on Mailbase, mostly targeted at the academic sector but relevant for non-academics too. These include Web-support, Web-support-siteserver and Website-info-mgt. At the time of writing this service is migrating to JISCMail (http://www.jiscmail.ac.uk) and details of the lists and their subscription instructions may alter: check the current details for each list on the JISCMail or Mailbase sites.

Market Position Newsletter (http://www.webposition.com)
A monthly newsletter about the latest developments in submitting to search engines and designing for ranking on search engines. The supporting web site exists mainly to promote the software product WebPosition Gold, which checks web pages for keywords and tags, and generates HTML to assist in ranking and submission. Both site and software are very useful for understanding the changing requirements of search engines, and for seeing which search engine powers which directory or index.

WebProNews (http://www.WebProNews.com)
A monthly newsletter containing one in-depth article on an aspect of web design or promotion. It is typically about search engine promotion and ranking design, but also covers other related topics. An archive of previous articles makes this a useful research site.

iEntry Network (http://www.ientry.com)
A network of e-mail newsletters (and supporting web sites) targeted at web site designers, managers and marketers. Newsletters include

WebProNews, FlashNewz, ComNewz, AdvertisingDay, DevNews and MacWebmasterFree, and each has a supporting site and archives.

Larry Chase's Web Digest For Marketers (http://wdfm.com)

This monthly newsletter has a different guest editor each month, who provides his or her top fifteen sites with a brief summary and analysis. It has more of a marketing focus than most, but usually includes sites that can provide useful ideas to site developers in terms of content and customer service. The free archive provides access to thousands of web site reviews from the past five years.

ADV-HTML (http://www.netsquirrel.com/adv-html)

This is a long-running and very effective skills-sharing site for web designers and developers. Questions submitted to the list are answered by other list members, and the questioner then submits a summary of the answers. This means that the archive of this list is an invaluable searchable source of troubleshooting and problem-solving advice.

The Search Engine Report (http://searchenginewatch.com/sereport/)

A monthly newsletter about search engines from Danny Sullivan, creator of the highly regarded Search Engine Watch web site. This newsletter provides current developments in search engine technology and policies, relevant both to web searchers and site owners. The comparisons, design advice and warnings in the newsletter, backed up by the best supporting site on the Web, and a full searchable archive, provide all the background information you could need.

Links to the web sites and services featured in the case studies and throughout this book can be found on the supporting web, site http://www.webtipsandtricks.co.uk

Bibliography

Douglas, N., Strengholt, G. and Velthoven, W., *Website Graphics Now,* London, Thames & Hudson, 1999

Ellsworth, J. and Ellsworth, M., *The New Internet Business Book,* New York, Wiley, 1996

Gallimore, A., *Developing an IT Strategy for your Library,* London, LA Publishing, 1997

Kerr, M., *How to Design Your Web Site Effectively,* London, Aslib, 1999

Lynch, P. and Horton, S. *Web Style Guide,* New Haven, Yale University Press, 1999

Nielsen, J., *Designing Web Usability,* Indianapolis, New Riders Publishing, 2000

Schwartz, E., *Webonomics,* London, Penguin, 1997

Segue Software, *Gain eConfidence,* Lexington, MA, Segue Software, 1999

Shafe, L., *Building Intranet Applications,* Burlington, MA, Intelligent Environments, 1996

Smith, M., *Internet Policy Handbook for Libraries,* New York, Neal-Schuman, 1999

Index